Best Easy Day Hikes
the Four Corners

Help Us Keep This Guide Up to Date

Every effort has been made by the author and editors to make this guide as accurate and useful as possible. However, many things can change after a guide is published—trails are rerouted, regulations change, techniques evolve, facilities come under new management, etc.

We would appreciate hearing from you concerning your experiences with this guide and how you feel it could be improved and kept up to date. While we may not be able to respond to all comments and suggestions, we'll take them to heart, and we'll also make certain to share them with the author. Please send your comments and suggestions to the following address:

Globe Pequot
Reader Response/Editorial Department
246 Goose Lane
Guilford, CT 06437

Or you may e-mail us at: editorial@falcon.com

Thanks for your input, and happy trails!

Best Easy Day Hikes Series

Best Easy Day Hikes the Four Corners

JD Tanner and Emily Ressler-Tanner

FALCONGUIDES

GUILFORD, CONNECTICUT

FALCONGUIDES®

An imprint of Rowman & Littlefield
Falcon and FalconGuides are registered trademarks and Make
Adventure Your Story is a trademark of Rowman & Littlefield.

Distributed by NATIONAL BOOK NETWORK

Copyright © 2017 by Rowman & Littlefield
Maps by Alena Pearce © Rowman & Littlefield

British Library Cataloguing-in-Publication Information Available

Library of Congress Control Number: 2016947423

ISBN 978-1-4930-2660-9 (paperback)
ISBN 978-1-4930-2661-6 (e-book)

∞™ The paper used in this publication meets the minimum require-
ments of American National Standard for Information Sciences—Perma-
nence of Paper for Printed Library Materials, ANSI/NISO Z39.48-1992.

The authors and Rowman & Littlefield assume no liability for acci-
dents happening to, or injuries sustained by, readers who engage
in the activities described in this book.

Contents

Acknowledgments viii

Introduction 1

How to Use This Guide 9

Trail Finder 11

Map Legend 13

THE HIKES

Arizona Region 14

  1. White House Trail: Canyon de Chelly
     National Monument 16

  2. Wildcat Trail: Monument Valley Navajo
     Tribal Park 20

Colorado Region 25

  3. Square Tower Trail: Hovenweep
     National Monument 27

  4. Sand Canyon Trail: Canyons of the
     Ancients National Monument............................ 31

  5. Spud (Potato) Lake Trail #661: San Juan
     National Forest 36

  6. Purgatory Trail #511: San Juan National Forest..... 40

  7. Colorado Trail: Southern Terminus Trailhead
     to Junction Creek Bridge.................................... 44

  8. Petroglyph Point Trail: Mesa Verde
     National Park.. 48

New Mexico Region 54

  9. Dancing Horse Trail: Four Corners Monument 56

  10. Anasazi Arch Trail: Bureau of Land Management .. 60

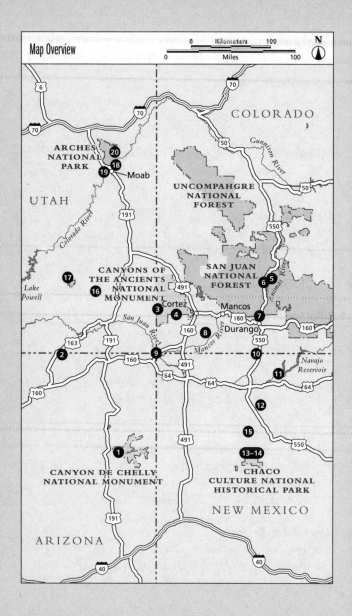

11. Simon Canyon Ruin Trail: Bureau of
    Land Management 64
12. Angel Peak Trail: Bureau of Land Management 68
13. Peñasco Blanco Trail: Chaco Culture National
    Historical Park 72
14. Pueblo Alto Trail: Chaco Culture National
    Historical Park 77
15. Bisti/De-Na-Zin Wilderness: Bureau of
    Land Management 82

Utah Region 86
16. House on Fire Ruin Trail: Bureau of
    Land Management 88
17. Sipapu and Kachina Bridges Loop Trail:
    Natural Bridges National Monument 92
18. Negro Bill Canyon Trail: Bureau of
    Land Management 97
19. Corona Arch Trail: Bureau of
    Land Management 101
20. Delicate Arch Trail: Arches National Park 105

About the Authors 110

Acknowledgments

We would like to send out a special thank-you to all the land managers who patiently answered our questions, pointed us toward the very best trails, and carefully reviewed the trail descriptions for this guide. We would also like to thank our friends and family for accompanying us on many of the trails in the Four Corners; your company, humor, support, and enthusiasm were very much appreciated. Finally, we would like to thank all of our friends at FalconGuides, particularly David Legere, Katie Benoit, Max Phelps, and Julie Marsh, for their support and encouragement, and for making a book out of our rough manuscript.

Introduction

The Four Corners region is a vast physiographic and geologic highland region located in the southwestern United States. The region includes much of southeastern Utah, southwestern Colorado, northwestern New Mexico, and northeastern Arizona. The boundaries of these four states intersect in a remote area of the Navajo Nation. The Four Corners gets its name from this quadripoint, which forms four right angles and is unique in that it is the only place in the United States where you can be in four states at the same time. The Four Corners Monument, one of several parks managed by Navajo Parks & Recreation, marks this distinctive landmark.

The area known collectively as the Four Corners region is part of the larger geographic area known as the Colorado Plateau. The Colorado Plateau covers over 130,000 square miles and is home to more National Park Service (NPS) units than any other region of the United States. Many of these NPS units are located in the Four Corners region and are highlighted in this guide, including Arches National Park, Mesa Verde National Park, Hovenweep National Monument, Natural Bridges National Monument, Canyons of the Ancients National Monument, Chaco Culture National Historical Park, and Canyon de Chelly National Monument.

The region is home to many tribal lands and nations, including the Navajo, Jicarilla Apache, Hopi, Southern Ute, Ute Mountain Ute, and Zuni. The largest of these entities is the Navajo Nation, which covers more than 27,000 square miles of land in the states of Arizona, Utah, and New Mexico.

We couldn't be more excited to introduce you to the extensive network of trails offered in the Four Corners region. Hiking opportunities are virtually unlimited in this region, and the landscape offers endless beauty and solitude for outdoor enthusiasts. Trails here follow towering sandstone cliffs, traverse quiet valleys and cool canyons, and climb over rough and rugged mountain terrain to some of the most spectacular scenery in the world. Those willing to venture to this hard-to-reach region will be rewarded with a multitude of recreational opportunities. Springs, arches, natural bridges, narrow canyons, ancient ruins, clear-flowing streams, and geologic wonders are the natural gems of the Four Corners, and are all highlighted in this guide.

If you are a visitor to the Four Corners, this collection of hiking trails will serve as a valuable tool for familiarizing yourself with the great variety of outdoor adventures within this vast region. Our hope is that this guide will serve as your introduction to the region's adventures, and will keep you returning to the Four Corners region time and time again. If you are a longtime local of the area, we hope this book will take you on some new adventures to some lesser-known trails in this diverse region.

This guide lists easy, moderate, and more challenging hikes in the Four Corners region. Some of the hikes can be found near the more populated towns of the region, including Moab, Utah; Durango, Colorado; and Farmington, New Mexico. Some trails are near the most popular vacation destinations, such as Mesa Verde and Arches National Parks, while others are located in more remote and seldom-visited areas, and will likely require a good bit of driving to reach the trailhead. All showcase the natural wonders hidden in this region. From views of majestic mountain peaks to hidden sandstone canyons, the hikes featured in the pages of this book are some of the best in the region. No matter where you choose to explore, you will be rewarded with brilliant memories and leave with a desire to return. Ask almost any outdoor enthusiast who has spent time here, and they will tell you that this rugged landscape has a way of getting a hold on your heart and soul.

We have done our best to include a little something for everyone, and have tried to select trails from many parts of the region while still making sure to include those trails widely considered to be superior for their scenic and historical significance. Hikes for families, for nature lovers, for scenic views, and for history buffs have all been included, and should be considered an introduction to the area and a starting point to continue your explorations in the Four Corners.

> May your trails be
> crooked, winding, lone-
> some, dangerous, leading
> to the most amazing
> view. May your moun-
> tains rise into and above
> the clouds.
>
> —Edward Abbey

This famous quote by American author and environmentalist Edward Abbey is the perfect way to start this guide. After all, Abbey used these words in his book *Desert Solitaire: A Season in the Wilderness*, which details Abbey's time in parts of the region, most notably Arches National Park. It is truly our wish to you that you find the areas in this guide as wonderful and wild as we have.

Weather

Hikers come to the Four Corners region year-round, but most come during spring, summer, and autumn. Since the region is a high desert environment, with daytime high temperatures often reaching 95°F to 105°F almost daily from June through August, summer is the most unfavorable time of the year to hike in the area. The exception is hikes at higher elevation ranges, where summer temperatures can be very mild.

Spring and autumn are the best hiking seasons for trips in the Four Corners region. Spring weather (March through May) can be highly variable, with daytime high temperatures ranging from the 50s to the 70s, and nighttime lows ranging from the 20s to 50s. Occasional cold fronts from the west and northwest can bring cold, windy conditions; rain showers at the lower elevations; and perhaps snow on the higher mesas, particularly in March and April. Snow will be present through early summer for all mountain hikes. Generally, warm, dry weather prevails between storm systems.

Early spring is one of the best times of the year to hike in the canyons of the region. Springs and seasonal streams are likely to be flowing, and slickrock water pockets will hold rainwater longer at this time of year, providing more flexibility and a margin of safety in the backcountry.

The onset of searing summer heat at lower elevations usually begins in late May, and it can persist into mid-September. Hikes at higher elevations may be quite pleasant. The monsoon season usually begins in mid-July and ends in mid-September. Moist tropical air masses over Mexico circulate an almost daily parade of thunderstorms over the region. Midsummer weather in the region can be characterized by heavy rainfall, which is usually accompanied by strong, gusty winds and lightning.

Autumn provides some of the most stable weather of the year. Clear, warm, sunny days and cool nights make this one of the most delightful seasons to visit the Four Corners region. Expect daytime highs to range from the 70s and 80s in September to the 40s and 50s by November. Overnight lows are typically range from the 20s to the 50s. Only the most active summer monsoon season will help recharge springs and streams, but the deepest water pockets often persist into early fall due to cooler temperatures and reduced evaporation. Cold fronts can sweep through the region as autumn progresses, and in some years, by mid- to late October, these fronts can drop temperatures significantly for several days or longer. Snowfall in the higher elevations, above 5,000 to 6,000 feet, is not uncommon.

Winter in the Four Corners region is cold and often windy, and deep snow sometimes covers the ground above 6,000 feet. To stay up to date on weather conditions, listen to local radio stations while driving, and check with Bureau of Land Management (BLM) and NPS offices for current forecasts. The National Oceanic and Atmospheric Administration is a good resource for current weather forecasts in the area (www.noaa.gov).

Rules and Regulations

The hiking trails in this book traverse through lands that are controlled and managed by various public agencies. Each group has its own rules and regulations that must be respected and adhered to at all times while hiking on these lands. The trails in this book cross through lands managed by the United States Forest Service, the National Park Service, state park systems, the Bureau of Land Management, and a couple of city park systems. Hikes on lands managed by the

NPS have firmer rules and regulations in regards to recreation and land-use restrictions.

When day hiking, you generally do not need permits to enjoy many of the trails in this book, although many land managers do request that you register at the trailhead. If you plan to embark on a long-distance hiking trip, you will want to call the managing office of the area you are hiking through and secure a backcountry permit for the area. You may be required to reserve your campsites for each night that you will be camping along the trail. The US Forest Service is typically less strict about camping and usually allows dispersed, primitive camping along trails as long as you are not within a particular distance from waterways, the trail, roads, and other specified areas. Before embarking on a hiking trip, plan ahead by checking the land manager's website or by calling the office of the management agency of the lands you will be traversing. They will provide the most up-to-date information on regulations and trail conditions.

Safety and Preparation

"Be prepared." The Boy Scouts say it, Leave No Trace says it, and the best outdoors people say it. Being prepared won't completely keep you out of harm's way when you're outdoors, but it will minimize the chances of finding yourself there. That being said, here are some things to consider:

- Speak with local land managers to get the most up-to-date information on road and trail conditions.
- Familiarize yourself with the basics of first aid (bites, stings, sprains, and breaks). Carry a first aid kit, and know how to use it.

- Hydrate! No matter where or when you are hiking, you should always carry water with you. A standard is two liters per person per day.

- Be prepared to treat water on longer hikes. Rivers and streams in the Four Corners area are not safe to drink directly from. Iodine tablets are small, light, and easy to carry.

- Carry a backpack to store the Ten Essentials: map, compass, sunglasses/sunscreen, extra food and water, extra clothes, headlamp/flashlight, first aid kit, fire starter, matches, and knife.

- Pack your cell phone (on vibrate) as a safety backup.

- Keep an eye on the kids. Having them carry a whistle, just in case, isn't the worst idea.

- Bring a leash, doggie bags, and extra water for your pets.

Leave No Trace

This hiking guide will take you to historical sites, conservation areas, national natural landmarks, and many other places of natural and cultural significance. For those reasons, the importance of Leave No Trace cannot be stressed enough. You are encouraged to carefully plan your trip so that you know as much as you possibly can about the area you will be visiting. Being aware of information such as the weather forecast, trail conditions, and water availability is an important factor in planning a successful trip.

Once you begin your hike, do your best to stick to trails so you do not inadvertently trample sensitive vegetation. Be prepared to pack out any trash that you bring with you, and remember, it never hurts to carry out trash that others may have left behind. Be extra careful when visiting sites of historical and natural importance. Leave everything as you found it, and never remove artifacts found in these sensitive areas.

Consider your impact on wildlife as you visit their homes, and be sure not to feed them, as this act is unhealthy for wildlife and dangerous for people. Respect other visitors and users by keeping your pets on a leash, stepping to the side of the trail to allow others to pass, and keeping noise to a minimum.

For more information on enjoying the outdoors responsibly, please visit the Leave No Trace Center for Outdoor Ethics website at www.LNT.org.

Visitor Information

More information about the hikes in this guide can be found by contacting the Trail Contact located in the hiking specifications at the beginning of each hike description.

How to Use This Guide

Each region begins with a section introduction, where you're given a sweeping look at the lay of the land. After this general overview, specific hikes within that region are described. You'll learn about the terrain and the surprises each route has to offer.

This guide is designed to be simple and easy to use. Each hike is described with a map and summary information that delivers the trail's vital statistics including length, difficulty, fees and permits, park hours, canine compatibility, and trail contacts. Directions to the trailhead are also provided, along with a general description of what you'll see along the way. A detailed route finder (Miles and Directions) sets forth mileages between significant landmarks along the trail.

How the Hikes Were Chosen

This guide describes trails that are accessible to almost every hiker, whether visiting from out of town or a local resident. The hikes in this guide range in length from just over 1 mile to over 12 miles, and most are in the 3- to 6-mile range. Hikes range in difficulty from flat excursions perfect for a family outing to more challenging treks in the Rocky Mountains. While these trails are among the best, keep in mind that nearby trails, sometimes in the same park or in a neighboring open space, may offer options better suited to your needs.

Selecting a Hike

Some would argue that no hike involving any kind of climbing is easy, but climbs are a fact of life in the Four Corners region. Trail difficulty is a highly subjective matter, but we've tried to give you an idea of what to expect on each hike. Below is a description of how trail difficulty is categorized in this guide.

Easy hikes are generally short and flat, taking no longer than an hour to complete.

Moderate hikes involve increased distance and relatively mild changes in elevation, and will take 1 to 2 hours to complete.

More challenging hikes feature some steep stretches, greater distances, and generally take longer than 2 hours to complete.

Keep in mind that what you think is easy is entirely dependent on your level of fitness and the adequacy of your gear (primarily shoes). Use the trail's length as a gauge of its relative difficulty—even if climbing is involved, it won't be too strenuous if the hike is less than 1 mile long. Some of the longer hikes are more strenuous than others due to length and elevation changes. If you are hiking with a group, select a hike that's appropriate for the least fit and prepared in your party.

Approximate hiking times are based on the assumption that on flat ground, most walkers average 2 miles per hour. Adjust that rate by the steepness of the terrain and your level of fitness (subtract time if you're an aerobic animal and add time if you're hiking with kids), and you have a ballpark hiking duration. Be sure to add more time if you plan to picnic or take part in other activities like bird-watching, swimming, wandering, or photography.

Trail Finder

Best Hikes for Lakes, Rivers, and Waterfalls

5   Spud (Potato) Lake Trail #661: San Juan National Forest

6   Purgatory Trail #511: San Juan National Forest

7   Colorado Trail: Southern Terminus Trailhead to Junction Creek Bridge

Best Hikes for Ruins

1   White House Trail: Canyon de Chelly National Monument

3   Square Tower Trail: Hovenweep National Monument

4   Sand Canyon Trail: Canyons of the Ancients National Monument

8   Petroglyph Point Trail: Mesa Verde National Park

13   Peñasco Blanco Trail: Chaco Culture National Historical Park

Best Hikes for Children

9   Dancing Horse Trail: Four Corners Monument

16   House on Fire Ruin Trail: Bureau of Land Management

Best Hikes for Great Views

2   Wildcat Trail: Monument Valley Navajo Tribal Park

12   Angel Peak Trail: Bureau of Land Management

18   Negro Bill Canyon Trail: Bureau of Land Management

20   Delicate Arch Trail: Arches National Park

Best Hikes for History Lovers

11   Simon Canyon Ruin Trail: Bureau of Land Management

14   Pueblo Alto Trail: Chaco Culture National Historical Park

Best Hikes for Nature Lovers

10   Anasazi Arch Trail: Bureau of Land Management

15   Bisti/De-Na-Zin Wilderness: Bureau of Land Management

17   Sipapu and Kachina Bridges Loop Trail: Natural Bridges National Monument

19   Corona Arch Trail: Bureau of Land Management

Map Legend

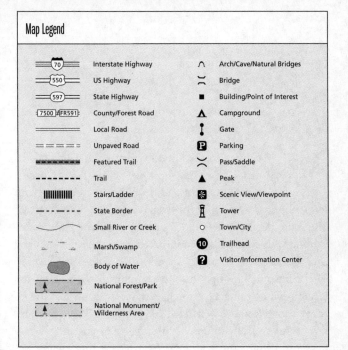

70 — Interstate Highway	∧ Arch/Cave/Natural Bridges
550 — US Highway	⏜ Bridge
597 — State Highway	■ Building/Point of Interest
7500 / FR591 — County/Forest Road	▲ Campground
— Local Road	╎ Gate
= = = = Unpaved Road	P Parking
▬▬▬ Featured Trail	⏝ Pass/Saddle
- - - - Trail	▲ Peak
‖‖‖‖‖‖‖ Stairs/Ladder	Scenic View/Viewpoint
- ·· - ·· State Border	Tower
∿ Small River or Creek	○ Town/City
Marsh/Swamp	10 Trailhead
Body of Water	? Visitor/Information Center
National Forest/Park	
National Monument/ Wilderness Area	

Arizona Region

Welcome to the Grand Canyon State! The northeastern Arizona portion of the Four Corners region is a vast and magnificent area filled with lofty buttes, towering cliffs, deep canyons, and spectacular blue skies. Most of the land is either Navajo or Hopi reservation. Both cultures have continued to take part in rich and ancient traditions centered on spiritual values, a connection to nature, and kinship. Driving through this region of the United States can feel a lot like traveling back in time, as many things have not changed for centuries. There are very few stores and restaurants in the smaller towns and villages scattered throughout the area. Visitors will find themselves driving for many miles from town to town. It is important to be prepared with food and water, and be sure to fill up the gas tank whenever possible.

The highlights of the Arizona region include mesmerizing rock formations, enormous river-carved canyons, a dry and arid climate, ancient ruins, and fantastic mesas that have been carved out of this rugged and challenging landscape over many, many years. In 2012 Arizona proudly boasted more than 10 million national park visits, which resulted in almost $750 million in economic benefit for the state from its twenty-two National Park Service–managed lands. Two of these parks are included in this guide and offer some of the most spectacular views and scenery in northeastern Arizona. Canyon de Chelly National Monument and Navajo National Monument are both located on the Navajo Nation reservation and offer a few self-guided hikes as well as several guided hikes.

The other trails found in the Arizona region are in the Navajo Nation Parks & Recreation system. Park offices are located in Window Rock, Arizona, capital of the Navajo Nation, the largest territory of a sovereign Native American nation in North America. Seven units are managed by the park system. This guide includes hikes in the Monument Valley Navajo Tribal Park and the Four Corners Monument (in the New Mexico chapter). These lands are very special and sacred to the Navajo people. Please respect and obey the rules and regulations that the land managers have implemented so that access to these beautiful places will continue. Hiking here seems to only be getting better!

1 White House Trail: Canyon de Chelly National Monument

The White House Trail offers hikers an amazing view of Canyon de Chelly and allows visitors a chance to experience what life was like several hundred years ago for the Puebloan people who inhabited the area. The 3-mile round-trip route takes hikers from the canyon rim to the canyon floor to visit the White House Ruins, and then back to the rim again.

Start: Southern end of the White House Overlook parking area
Distance: 3.0 miles out and back
Hiking time: 2 to 3 hours
Difficulty: Moderate due to gradual ascent on the return
Trail surface: Slickrock, sand, and packed-dirt
Best season: Fall and spring
Other trail users: None

Canine compatibility: No dogs permitted
Fees and permits: None
Schedule: Open year-round
Maps: USGS Chinle AZ; park map and brochure available at the visitor center
Trail contact: Canyon de Chelly National Monument, PO Box 588, Chinle, AZ 86503; (928) 674-5500; www.nps.gov/cach

Finding the trailhead: From the Canyon de Chelly National Monument visitor center, drive 5.0 miles on South Rim Drive. Turn left (north) toward the White House Overlook and drive another 0.6 mile to the parking area. GPS: N36 7.830' / W109 28.655'

The Hike

It took millions of years of land uplifts and water erosion to create Canyon de Chelly. Because of the constant water

```
    #440  08-28-2018 2:28PM
  Item(s) checked out to p12650882.

TITLE: The broken girls
BARCODE: 37653022567385
DUE DATE: 09-19-18

TITLE: Southernmost : a novel
BARCODE: 37653022904620
DUE DATE: 09-19-18

TITLE: Complete plays.
BARCODE: 37653003650465
DUE DATE: 09-25-18

TITLE: Best easy day hikes : the Four Co
BARCODE: 37653021736957
DUE DATE: 09-25-18

TITLE: A portrait of the artist as a you
BARCODE: 37653016057674
DUE DATE: 09-25-18

TITLE: The witches of New York : a novel
BARCODE: 37653022280567
DUE DATE: 09-19-18
```

flow, rich soil has continued to make its way into the canyon and has allowed for productive croplands and grazing for animals. The Ancient Puebloans who originally settled in the canyon built pit houses, but eventually began to build their homes in the alcoves of the canyon walls to take advantage of the sunlight and natural protection. These people prospered until the mid-1300s; they eventually left the canyons to seek better farmlands.

President Herbert Hoover designated the canyon as a national monument in 1931. Today the monument covers about 84,000 acres on land within the Navajo Nation reservation, and is still home to around forty families, many living in the canyon. The park service and the Navajo Nation work together to preserve the area, as it is a sacred place to the Navajo and holds much history. Local guiding services offer in-depth and informational tours into the canyon to those who are interested. The White House Trail is the only trail in the park that does not require a guide and is open to the public. The park does offer ranger-led hikes and activities, and there are even several overlooks located along the canyon rim that the public can drive to for views down into the canyon. Spider Rock Overlook is highly recommended before or after the hike.

The hike begins at the White House Overlook, about 6 miles from the visitor center. Locate the trailhead at the southern end of the overlook and parking area, and begin hiking south on the slickrock along the canyon rim. There are excellent views all along the canyon rim, including a view of the White House Ruins before you leave for the hike and a great look east into the canyon at 0.1 mile. At 0.3 mile the trail turns left (east) and begins to descend into the canyon along the rocky and dirt-packed trail. There are several rock formations to check out and enjoy on the hike down the canyon wall, including a man-made cave at 1.0 mile.

Not long after passing through the cave, you will reach the canyon floor and continue hiking north along the trail. There are some private property areas to respect along the canyon floor. At 1.2 miles you will cross over the Chinle Wash on a small footbridge and turn left (north) to continue toward the ruins. Reach the ruins at 1.5 miles. There is a fence here to keep people from entering the ruins, as they are a sacred place to the Navajo. Across the wash (southwest) are restrooms and a small recreation area where people can picnic and relax before the return hike. Return to the park-

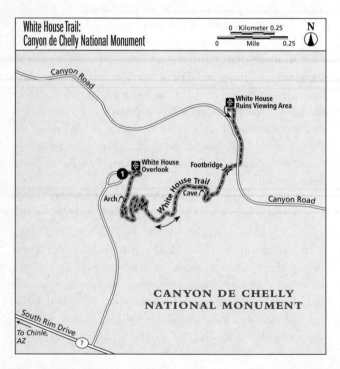

ing area and trailhead via the same route. Keep in mind that the hike back up the canyon wall can be strenuous for some people. Bring plenty of water and take advantage of the seating and rest areas during the hot summer months.

Miles and Directions

0.0 From the trailhead begin hiking south on the White House Trail.

0.1 Come to an overlook offering views east into the canyon.

0.3 The trail turns east and begins descending into the canyon.

1.0 The trail travels through a man-made cave.

1.1 Come to the canyon floor and continue hiking north.

1.2 Cross a small footbridge over Chinle Wash and then turn left (north).

1.5 Reach the White House Ruins viewing area. Retrace your steps to the trailhead.

3.0 Arrive back at the parking area after returning via the same route.

2 Wildcat Trail: Monument Valley Navajo Tribal Park

The Wildcat Trail is 4-mile lollipop hike into one of the most scenic areas that the Four Corners has to offer. Monument Valley has been the backdrop for a long list of films and television shows. This trail lets hikers feel like they stepped back in time into the Wild West. Hikers will travel around one of the "Mittens," famous rock buttes in the park, and will, at one point, find themselves standing in a spot where three towering buttes surround them.

Start: Wildcat Trail trailhead sign at the northwest corner of the visitor center parking area
Distance: 4.0-mile lollipop
Hiking time: 2 to 3 hours
Difficulty: Moderate due to sandy sections
Trail surface: Sand, dirt, and rock
Best season: Spring and fall
Other trail users: Horseback riders
Canine compatibility: Leashed dogs permitted

Fees and permits: Park entry fee
Schedule: Open year round; check website for closures
Maps: USGS Rooster Rock AZ-UT; trail map available at the park visitor center
Trail contact: Navajo Nation Parks and Recreation, PO Box 2520, Window Rock, AZ 86515; (928) 871-6647; http://navajo nationparks.org/navajo-tribal -parks/monument-valley-navajo -tribal-park/

Finding the trailhead: From Mexican Hat, Utah, drive west on US 163 for 20.5 miles to Monument Valley Road. Turn left (southeast) onto Monument Valley Road, drive 3.9 miles to the visitor center parking area, and park in the northwest corner of the lot. The trailhead is just a short walk on Indian Route 42. GPS: N36 59.120'/W110 6.801'

The Hike

Monument Valley Navajo Tribal Park, known by the Navajo as Tse'Bii'Ndzisgaii, might be one of the most photographed places on earth. The valley is host to towering sandstone rock formations that have been sculpted over time and soar 400 to 1,000 feet above the valley floor. Combined with the surrounding mesas, buttes, and desert environment, it truly is one of the natural wonders of the world. The park covers almost 92,000 acres in northern Arizona and southern Utah, lies within the Navajo Nation reservation, and is managed by the Navajo Nation Parks & Recreation department.

Most have heard the basic science of an area like Monument Valley. Basically, over millions of years, layers upon layers of sediments settled and cemented in a basin. The basin lifted up and became a plateau as the natural forces of wind and water slowly removed the softer materials and exposed what we see before us today. The spires, buttes, and other formations are still slowly being chipped away, but will be around long after we are gone. The formations in Monument Valley have become more and more famous as they have been seen in the backdrops of many movies and television shows, beginning with several John Wayne films. The visitor center offers museums, souvenirs, restrooms, a restaurant, a lodge, and much more. Guided tours of the park are available by vehicle and by horseback. The Wildcat Trail is the only self-guided trail in the park, but offers some world-class scenery as it takes hikers for a walk through the world-famous Mitten Buttes and Merrick Butte.

After parking in the northwest section of the main parking area, walk north along Indian Route 42 for a short distance and follow the road as it turns right (east). The Wildcat

Trail trailhead is at the northeast corner of the road inter-section. Begin hiking north on the sandy trail as it slowly descends to the valley floor. The trail passes numerous rental cabins that face out toward the buttes as well, a great place to stay for the night. This section of the trail has some very sandy sections and may be a little challenging on the return hike. At 0.7 mile reach the loop portion of the hike and stay right (southeast) to follow the park's preferred direction of travel. The trail to the left (northeast) is the return trail.

As this portion of the hike begins, hikers will navigate through an area where the well-worn trail joins the wash and/or crosses the wash a time or two. Again, the trail is well worn and beginner navigation skills are all that are required. At 1.7 miles you will find yourself standing in the center of the two Mitten Buttes and Merrick Butte for a great pan-orama. Here the trail also joins a two-wheel-drive road for a short section. The road leads to private residences. At 1.8 miles veer left (northwest) off the road and back onto the narrow footpath.

The trail continues along the valley floor through the desert shrublands and slowly circles northwest and then west around the westernmost Mitten Butte. The trail drops down into a large wash at 2.7 miles and continues in the wash for a short distance to 2.8 miles, where it exits the wash to the left (southwest). Hike up over a small hill and then back down to complete the loop portion of the hike at 3.3 miles. Turn right (west) to return to the trailhead and parking area via the same route at 4.0 miles.

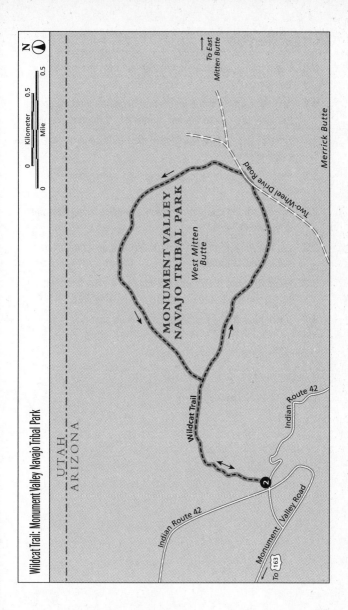

Wildcat Trail: Monument Valley Navajo Tribal Park

Miles and Directions

0.0 Begin hiking north on the Wildcat Trail from the signed trailhead.

0.7 Stay right (east) at the junction to begin the loop portion of the hike. The trail to the left (northeast) is the return trail.

1.7 The trail joins a two-wheel-drive road for a short stretch while heading north.

1.8 Veer left (northwest) to leave the road and continue on the footpath.

2.7 The trail drops down into a wash. Continue hiking southwest in the wash.

2.8 Exit the wash to the left (southwest) and continue hiking on the narrow footpath.

3.3 Reach the end of the loop portion of the hike. Turn right (west) to return to the trailhead and parking area.

4.0 Arrive back at the trailhead and parking area.

Colorado Region

Welcome to Colorful Colorado! The southwestern Colorado portion of the Four Corners region is an awe-inspiring and diverse area filled with desert mesas, majestic mountains, deep canyons, and quaint mountain towns. Part of the land is Ute reservation, but a majority is public land. Mountain biking, ice climbing, mountaineering, whitewater rafting, kayaking, horseback riding, and, of course, hiking are part of a laundry list of things people can do in southwestern Colorado. Unlike in northeastern Arizona, there is a larger selection of stores and restaurants in the small towns that are scattered throughout the area, such as Cortez, Durango, Telluride, and Ouray.

Visitors to the area may find themselves driving and/or hiking at high elevations. The highest elevation for a hike in this region is more than 14,000 feet. Driving over passes at 9,000 to 10,000 feet is not uncommon. Be prepared by drinking plenty of water before arriving and while in the area.

The highlights of the Colorado region include classic Rocky Mountains, enormous river-carved canyons, a dry and arid climate, ancient ruins, and fantastic mesas that have been carved out of this rugged and challenging landscape over eons. Six of the trails in this book are scattered throughout this mountainous area.

When people think of outdoor meccas in the lower forty-eight states, Colorado usually makes the list. However, many people tend to make their way to Denver because of the easier access via plane. Southwestern Colorado is a little tougher to get to but well worth the effort once you see how many fewer people there are. National parks in the area and included in this guide are Mesa Verde National Park, Hovenweep National Monument, and Canyons of the Ancients National Monument. Other parks nearby include the Black Canyon of the Gunnison National Park, Great Sand Dunes National Park & Preserve, Colorado National Monument, and Chimney Rock National Monument. Other trails in the Colorado region are located in Bureau of Land Management, US Forest Service, Colorado state, and City of Durango park systems.

In this region, hikers will find themselves in the canyons of western Colorado and along rivers that offer world-class trout fishing. They will follow historic trails like the Colorado Trail. Like many of the mountainous areas of Colorado, the southwest is known for its rich mining history. The lower elevations in the far southwest are scattered with old ruins like those found in Mesa Verde National Park, which hosts some of the most notable and well-preserved ruins in the United States.

3 Square Tower Trail: Hovenweep National Monument

The Square Tower Trail in Hovenweep National Monument is an excellent adventure for families. This 1.75-mile round-trip hike takes hikers for a short journey around the rim of Little Ruin Canyon, and offers beautiful views of the ruins located in the canyon as well as of the surrounding area. Take advantage of one of few national park facilities that allows pets on the trails.

Start: To the south behind the visitor center
Distance: 1.75-mile lollipop
Hiking time: About 2 hours
Difficulty: Easy
Trail surface: Pavement, packed dirt, and slickrock
Best season: Fall through spring
Other trail users: None
Canine compatibility: Leashed dogs permitted

Fees and permits: Park entrance fee required at visitor center
Schedule: Open year-round
Maps: USGS Negro Canyon CO; trail map available in the park office
Trail contact: Hovenweep National Monument, McElmo Rte., Cortez, CO 81321; (970) 562-4282; www.nps.gov/hove

Finding the trailhead: From Cortez, Colorado, turn west onto CR G and drive 29.8 miles to Reservation Road. Turn right (north) onto Reservation Road and drive 9.5 miles to Hovenweep Road. Turn right (east) onto Hovenweep Road/CR 212 and drive 0.9 mile to Hovenweep Campground Road. Turn right (southeast) onto Hovenweep Campground Road/CR 268A and drive 0.3 mile to the visitor center and parking area. GPS: N37 23.142'/W109 4.517'

The Hike

Hovenweep National Monument is located on the border of Colorado and Utah, equidistant from the towns of Blanding, Utah; Bluff, Utah; and Cortez, Colorado. The remoteness of this park makes it an unlikely place to just stumble upon. Those who visit really want to be here, and they have good reason: The site's rich cultural history coupled with the raw, high desert beauty of the landscape make Hovenweep National Monument a worthy destination. The monument is also reliably less crowded than its neighbor to the east, Mesa Verde National Park, making it a good choice for folks hoping to escape busy trails.

According to park literature, humans have been visiting this area for more than 10,000 years. The first known people who used this land were nomadic hunters and gatherers. Eventually people began to settle here. These people, known as Ancestral Puebloans, planted crops, including beans, corn, and squash, and built the towers found at this site between AD 500 and 1300, with the majority of the masonry being completed between AD 1200 and 1300. It seems that the site was abandoned by the end of the thirteenth century. Drought, warfare, and depletion of natural resources are several of the hardships that historians and archaeologists believe encouraged the Ancestral Puebloans to leave this area.

The Square Tower Trail is an excellent choice for people wanting to view the unique towerlike ruins found in Hovenweep National Monument. Despite its relatively short distance, the Square Tower Trail visits many distinctive ruins and offers lovely desert scenery. The route begins just behind the visitor center and heads south along a paved walking trail. Along this portion of the trail, look for common plants of the Colorado Plateau, such as Mormon tea, Utah juniper, and cliffrose. Several interpretive signs point out and describe these plants. At 0.2 mile the paved portion of the trail ends at the rim of Little Ruin Canyon. Turn right (northwest) onto the dirt/rock path to hike the loop in a counterclockwise direction. After a very short distance, the trail passes a fortresslike ruin known as Stronghold House.

At 0.5 mile you come to a fork in the trail. Turn left (south) onto the Tower Point Loop Trail to visit the Tower Point Ruin. At Tower Point at 0.6 mile, enjoy great views of Little Ruin Canyon. Look just below the rim of the

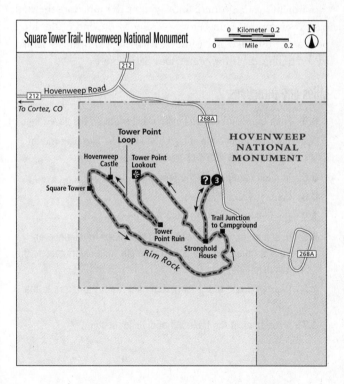

canyon to view several alcoves that were used by the Ancestral Puebloans to store crops. At 0.8 mile you will come to the ruin known as Hovenweep Castle, and shortly thereafter is a good view of Square Tower, a large, two-story ruin located down in the canyon.

At 1.2 miles pass several more ruins before the trail curves to the north and descends into Little Ruin Canyon at 1.3 miles. Continue northward and cross the canyon, coming to a trail junction at 1.5 miles shortly after reaching the north rim of the canyon. Turn left (northwest) to continue on the Square Tower Trail. The trail to the right (northeast) leads to the monument's campground. Shortly after the junction, the trail passes yet another ruin before coming to the end of the loop portion of the hike at 1.6 miles. Turn right (north) to return to the trailhead, visitor center, and parking area.

Miles and Directions

0.0 From the visitor center, begin hiking south on the paved trail.

0.2 The paved trail ends at Little Ruin Canyon. Turn right (northwest) onto the dirt/rock path.

0.5 Turn left (south) onto the Tower Point Loop Trail.

0.6 Come to Tower Point.

1.3 The trail descends into Little Ruin Canyon.

1.5 Reach a trail junction. Stay left (northwest) to continue on Square Tower Trail. The trail to the right (northeast) goes to the campground.

1.6 Reach the end of the loop. Turn right (north) to return to the start.

1.75 Arrive back at the trailhead and visitor center.

4 Sand Canyon Trail: Canyons of the Ancients National Monument

The Sand Canyon Trail in the Canyons of the Ancients National Monument offers numerous recreational opportunities to locals as well as to visitors to the area. Hikers, bikers, and horseback riders all enjoy the 13.2-mile out-and-back trail and the surrounding area. Hikers choosing to explore this area will find numerous cliff dwellings located in Sand Canyon, and will have beautiful views of Sleeping Ute Mountain on the return hike.

Start: Sand Canyon South Trailhead

Distance: 13.2 miles out and back

Hiking time: 7 to 8 hours

Difficulty: More challenging due to length

Trail surface: Dirt, rock, slickrock, and sand

Best season: Fall through spring

Other trail users: Bikers, horseback riders

Canine compatibility: Leashed dogs permitted

Fees and permits: None

Schedule: Open year-round

Maps: USGS Roggen CO; trail map available at the Anasazi Heritage Center near Dolores, Colorado

Trail contact: Canyons of the Ancients National Monument and Anasazi Heritage Center, 27501 CO 184, Dolores, CO 81323; (970) 882-5600; www.blm.gov/co/st/en/nm/canm.html

Finding the trailhead: From Cortez, Colorado, drive 12.1 miles on CR G to the Sand Canyon South Trailhead and parking area on the right (north) side of the road. GPS: N37 20.494' / W108 49.066'

The Hike

The Canyons of the Ancients National Monument is over-seen by the Bureau of Land Management and includes almost 171,000 acres of land in southwestern Colorado. The site has more than 6,000 recorded archaeological sites, and in some places there are as many as 100 sites per square mile. Researchers believe that several families came together around AD 1250 at the head of Sand Canyon, built a large, protective, U-shaped wall curving to the north, and then built hundreds of square rooms and round kivas within the wall. Community structures, plazas, and even a great kiva were built in this space. By 1275 it is believed that the Sand Canyon ruins were about three times the size of the Cliff Palace ruins found in Mesa Verde National Park. Not long after this prosperous period came a series of events that ended the growth of Sand Canyon.

In 1276 a severe drought hit the area and caused many of the crops to fail—and pushed most of the wildlife out of the area as well. Many of the residents suffered enough that they packed up and left for better living conditions. Still, many more stayed to live through the harsh conditions. Then, in 1277, it is believed that another tribe attacked the people of Sand Canyon—probably a neighboring tribe that was suffering from the drought as well. The survivors from this attack packed up their belongings and moved on to other places. Native Americans from the area say that the spirits of the ancestors have been the only inhabitants of the ruins for more than 700 years.

Many people travel to the monument today to bike ride, ride horses, and hike. The trail systems here allow for all three modes of travel, and most are marked to let people know which modes are allowed on each trail. There are no services at the trailhead except a portable outhouse and an informational kiosk at the parking area.

Begin hiking north from the Sand Canyon South Trailhead and parking area on the slickrock trail that has been marked well with rock cairns. The trail circles around to the left (west) of a large rock formation and then reaches a side trail at 0.2 mile. To the right (east), the short trail leads to the first set of small ruins along the route. Continue left (northeast) on the main trail as the slickrock ends at around 0.3 mile and the trail becomes a mix of sand and packed dirt.

At 0.7 mile you will come to the first of several ruins of cliff dwellings. There are numerous sets of ruins along this route, and they will not all be pointed out in this guide as most are visible from the trail. Continue right (northeast) along the trail as it continues up the canyon. You will reach a trail junction at 1.7 miles. The trail to the left (west) connects to the East Rock Creek Trail; continue right (north) on the Sand Canyon Trail.

Sand Canyon slowly narrows as you continue to hike north. At 3.6 miles you will see a sign that reads "Foot Traffic Only." The canyon becomes much narrower at this point, and you eventually reach a section of trail that begins switchbacking up the canyon wall on the west side at 4.3 miles. A series of switchbacks will take you higher and higher up the canyon wall, and offers great views to the south of Sleeping Ute Mountain.

Reach the end of the switchbacks at 5.1 miles, and continue hiking northward in what has now become a pine-forested area that provides a bit more shade. Hike through the beautifully forested high plains desert until you reach a steep climb at 6.4 miles. Hike up the steep hill, which

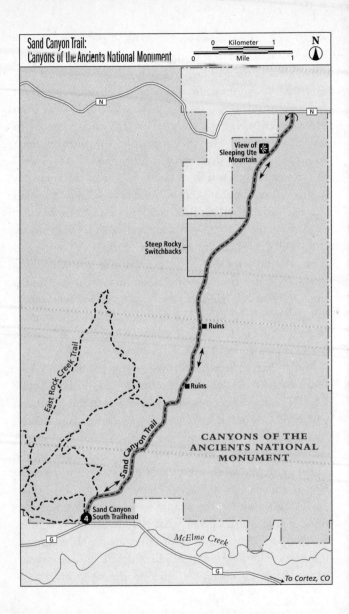

Sand Canyon Trail:
Canyons of the Ancients National Monument

N

0   Kilometer   1
0   Mile   1

N

View of
Sleeping Ute
Mountain

Steep Rocky
Switchbacks

Ruins

Ruins

Sand Canyon Trail

East Rock Creek Trail

CANYONS OF THE
ANCIENTS NATIONAL
MONUMENT

4 Sand Canyon
South Trailhead

G

McElmo Creek

G

To Cortez, CO

includes a couple of switchbacks and then eventually flattens out as you arrive at the Sand Canyon North Trailhead at 6.6 miles. Turn around here and return to the Sand Canyon South Trailhead and parking area via the same route.

Miles and Directions

0.0 Begin hiking north from the Sand Canyon South Trailhead and parking area on the slickrock trail marked with rock cairns.

0.2 Continue left (north) up the main trail. A trail to the right (east) leads to the first ruins.

0.3 The slickrock ends and the trail becomes sand and packed dirt.

0.7 Stay right (northeast); a trail to the left (northwest) leads to ruins.

1.7 Reach a trail junction with a connector trail that leads to the East Rock Creek Trail on the left (west). Continue hiking north on the Sand Canyon Trail.

3.6 Come to a sign that reads "Foot Traffic Only" as Sand Canyon begins to narrow.

4.3 Begin hiking up a series of switchbacks on the west side of the canyon.

5.1 Reach the top of the switchbacks and continue hiking north.

6.4 Hike up a steep section of trail.

6.6 Arrive at the Sand Canyon North Trailhead and parking area. Turn around here to return via the same route.

13.2 Arrive back at the Sand Canyon South Trailhead and parking area.

5 Spud (Potato) Lake Trail #661: San Juan National Forest

Known by locals as Spud Lake, Potato Lake is a great family adventure. Be sure to grab a fishing pole (and permit) for this hike. Potato Lake offers beautiful mountain scenery at a high-altitude fishing pond. The lake sits at the base of Spud Mountain and offers hikers hours upon hours of hiking, exploring, fishing, and relaxing options.

Start: Spud (Potato) Lake Trailhead and parking area north of the lily pad–covered lake
Distance: 2.4 miles out and back
Hiking time: 2 to 3 hours
Difficulty: Moderate due to length
Trail surface: Forested trail
Best season: Year-round
Other trail users: Horseback riders

Canine compatibility: Leashed dogs permitted
Fees and permits: None
Schedule: Open year-round
Maps: USGS Engineer Mountain CO
Trail contact: San Juan National Forest, 15 Burnett Ct., Durango, CO 81301; (970) 247-4874; www.fs.usda.gov/main/sanjuan/home

Finding the trailhead: From Durango, Colorado, drive about 28.5 miles north on US 550 and turn right (south) onto FR 591/Lime Creek Road. Drive 2.9 miles to a parking area on the left (north) side of the road. GPS: N37 39.161'/W107 46.409'

The Hike

The San Juan National Forest is southwestern Colorado's gateway to adventure, and includes approximately 1.8

million acres of federal lands managed by the US Forest Service. There is an amazing range of scenery in this part of the Four Corners region. Near the actual Four Corners, Colorado consists of high desert mesas and canyons, and as you travel east into the state, you encounter majestic alpine peaks and meadows. The San Juan National Forest features a scenic byway, the San Juan Skyway, and a Bureau of Land Management four-wheel-drive scenic byway, the Alpine Loop Back Country Byway. Visitors come here for the same reason that the locals live here: They can enjoy a variety of outdoor activities including hiking, mountain biking, hunting, fishing, skiing, horseback riding, and camping. The San Juan National Forest also shares management duties of three designated wilderness areas: the Weminuche Wilderness, the Lizard Head Wilderness, and the South San Juan Wilderness.

You will see many maps and other guides refer to this trail as the Potato Lake Trail. Because the forest service web page refers to it as Spud Lake Trail, we refer to it as Spud Lake Trail in this guide.

Once you've located the unsigned parking area on the north side of FR 591/Lime Creek Road, directly north of a decent-size lily pad–covered lake, begin hiking north on the packed-dirt and rocky trail to the northeast of the parking area. The trailhead is at approximately 9,400 feet, and the trail will gain about 400 vertical feet by the time you've arrived at Spud Lake. Hiking north, you will pass through a beautiful aspen grove as the trail gradually climbs the uphill grade and levels out for a short distance at 0.3 mile. At 0.5 mile begin the gradual climb again. The trail becomes a bit rockier, and passes a beaver pond on the left (north) at 0.7 mile. Continue hiking east and then north as the trail finishes up its last uphill and arrives at Potato (Spud) Lake at 1.2 miles, with

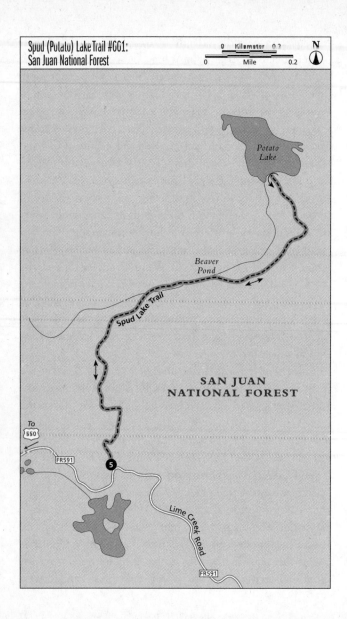

Kilometer 0.2

0   Mile   0.2

N

Potato
Lake

Beaver
Pond

Spud Lake Trail

SAN JUAN
NATIONAL FOREST

To
550

FR591

5

Lime Creek Road

FR591

Potato Hill looming in the background. After a little fishing, relaxing, or a stroll around the lake, return to the trailhead and parking area via the same route.

Miles and Directions

0.0 Begin hiking north on the rocky trail just east of the parking area.

0.3 After heading gradually uphill through an aspen grove, the trail begins to level out.

0.5 The trail begins a gradual climb again.

0.7 Pass a small beaver pond on the left (north).

1.2 Arrive at Potato (Spud) Lake. Return to the trailhead and parking area via the same route.

2.4 Arrive back at the trailhead and parking area.

6 Purgatory Trail #511: San Juan National Forest

This 3.8-mile out-and-back trail takes hikers through beautiful aspen groves down to an area known as Purgatory Flats. Once at the Flats, hikers can enjoy time along Cascade Creek or extend their hike on the Animas River Trail. This area is also a popular place for bird-watching and offers a great fall foliage hike through the aspens.

Start: Purgatory Trail trailhead on the south side of Tacoma Drive

Distance: 3.8 miles out and back

Hiking time: 2 to 3 hours

Difficulty: Moderate due to length and rugged terrain

Trail surface: Packed dirt; rocky and forested

Best season: From Sept to Nov for the fall foliage

Other trail users: Horseback riders

Canine compatibility: Leashed dogs permitted

Fees and permits: None

Schedule: Open year-round

Maps: USGS Engineer Mountain CO; National Geographic Trails Illustrated #140 and #144

Trail contact: San Juan National Forest, 15 Burnett Ct., Durango, CO 81301; (970) 247-4874; www.fs.usda.gov/main/sanjuan/home

Finding the trailhead: From Durango, Colorado, drive about 26.5 miles north on US 550 and turn right (south) onto Tacoma Drive. Drive 0.2 mile on Tacoma Drive to a parking area on the left (north) side of the road. GPS: N37 37.780'/W107 48.392'

The Hike

The Purgatory Trail is a great day-trip trail that winds down through a beautiful aspen forest and then pops out alongside

Cascade Creek. The area down in the valley is a popular place for overnight camping or makes a great rest stop for hikers out on a longer journey. The trail begins directly across from the entrance to the Purgatory Resort, a beautiful place to spend the night if you are staying in the area. The resort is a great base camp for those looking to "camp" in style while enjoying everything that the area has to offer, including world-class mountain biking, world-class trout fishing, hiking and camping, and the Million Dollar Highway, the section of US 550 from Silverton to Ouray.

The trail drops quickly to Purgatory Flats, an open grassy valley 1 mile below the highway. Purgatory Flats is a historical grazing area, so don't be surprised to see cattle down in the valley when you arrive. You'll want to get a fishing permit and bring your rod and reel for this one, if you fish. Lime Creek and Cascade Creek converge here and offer good trout fishing.

From the trailhead on the south side of Tacoma Drive, begin hiking southeast on the packed-dirt and rocky trail. At 0.1 mile you will reach the Weminuche Wilderness kiosk and trail register. Be sure to register yourself and your group, as it helps the land managers track usage and could be used to help track you should you get lost. Continue hiking southeast from the register as the trail begins its descent down the west side of the valley wall. Come to a small but easily rock-hopped creek crossing at 0.4 mile. The trail continues to descend through a beautiful aspen grove. Time your hike just right in the fall, and you are in for quite a treat, as this entire area is known for its fall foliage beauty.

At 0.9 mile the trail circles south to a great little overlook area that provides views south down toward Cascade Canyon. The trail continues its half circle so that you are

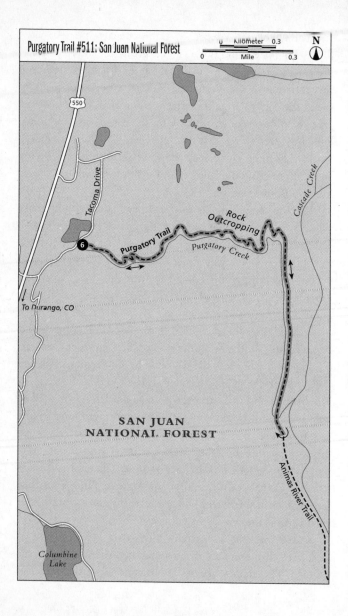

hiking north for a short distance before coming to a short series of switchbacks that finish the descent and end at the valley floor at 1.2 miles. This descent was by no means the steepest one in the area or in this guide, but don't let it fool you, and remember that you'll need the energy to hike back up on the way back. Once on the valley floor, you can see a few camping areas to the east and north in the forested areas of the Flats. Continue hiking south on the Purgatory Trail out onto the Purgatory Flats. Arrive at a great rest area along Cascade Creek just before entering Cascade Canyon at 1.9 miles. Though the trail continues for several miles south into the canyon, this is the turnaround point for this recommended hike.

Miles and Directions

0.0 From the trailhead on the south side of Tacoma Drive, begin hiking south.

0.1 Reach the Weminuche Wilderness kiosk and trail register.

0.4 Reach a small creek crossing.

0.9 Reach a nice overlook area on the right that looks down into Purgatory Flats.

1.2 The descent ends, and you arrive at the Flats.

1.9 Arrive at Cascade Creek. Return to the trailhead and parking area via the same route.

3.8 Arrive back at the trailhead and parking area.

7 Colorado Trail: Southern Terminus Trailhead to Junction Creek Bridge

Welcome to the southern terminus of the Colorado Trail! This 5.4-mile out-and-back section of the trail will give all the thru-hike dreamers a small taste of what the trail has to offer. The trail travels along Junction Creek and offers numerous areas to enjoy the nice cool mountain runoff during the warm mountain summer days.

Start: Colorado Trail Durango trailhead and parking area

Distance: 5.4 miles out and back

Hiking time: About 3 hours

Difficulty: Moderate due to length and some steep climbs

Trail surface: Packed dirt; forested

Best season: Spring through fall

Other trail users: Bikers and horseback riders

Canine compatibility: Leashed dogs permitted

Fees and permits: None

Schedule: Open year-round

Maps: USGS Durango West CO; trail map available at www.colora dotrail.org

Trail contact: San Juan National Forest, 15 Burnett Ct., Durango, CO 81301; (970) 247-4874; www.fs.usda.gov/sanjuan

Finding the trailhead: From Durango, Colorado, drive north on Main Avenue for 1.1 miles. Turn left (west) onto West 25th Street. Continue 0.2 mile on West 25th Street to a slight right; the road becomes Junction Street. Drive 0.9 mile on Junction Street and then stay left onto CR 204/Junction Creek Road. After 2.5 miles turn left (west) into the parking area and trailhead. GPS: N37 19.882'/W107 54.176'

The Hike

The Colorado Trail idea was conceived back in 1973 by Bill Lucas and Merrill Hastings. Since that time the trail has become an established, marked, and mostly nonmotorized trail open to hikers, horse riders, and bicyclists. From Waterton Canyon near Denver, the trail makes its way for almost 500 miles from the Front Range over the Rockies, through the state's most mountainous regions, to the outskirts of Durango. Thru-hikers taking on the entire trail pass through eight mountain ranges, six national forests, and six wilderness areas. Trail elevations range from about 5,500 feet at Denver to a high of 13,271 feet in the San Juan Mountains.

Passing through some of the state's most beautiful country, the trail allows an abundance of wildlife and wildflower viewing and photography. In addition to offering stunning natural scenery, the trail also passes through historic mining towns, ski resorts, and quaint mountain towns. The western portion of the trail tends to see less human impact, as this side of the mountains and the Four Corners area continue to be more challenging to reach by plane and vehicle. The southern terminus section described here does not give hikers a good feel for the high-altitude hiking they would experience on other sections of the trail, but the beautiful scenery and the opportunity to just get your feet on the trail is enough to get serious hikers thinking about the possibilities of a thru-hike.

From the Colorado Trail trailhead and parking area, begin hiking northwest on the packed-dirt trail. The trailhead area has a pit toilet that closes in the late fall and may still be closed in early spring. There is also a nice information kiosk at the trailhead for those interested in the information or, more importantly, the photo op.

For the entire section described here, the trail parallels Junction Creek until the turnaround point at Junction Creek Bridge. At 0.2 mile cross a small footbridge over a drainage that runs into Junction Creek and continue hiking northwest. The trail begins a slow and gradual climb on the right (north) side of the valley, and passes numerous areas to stop and enjoy the cool waters of Junction Creek. At mile 1.1 there is a great place to pull off to the left side of the trail and sit by the creek, or even cool your feet during those warm summer months.

Continue hiking northwest from here, and reach another trail access point on the right (north) at 1.2 miles. The forest is thick with ponderosa pine, fir, and spruce trees. There is a parking area, a trail kiosk, and access to the Junction Creek Campground just up the road from this point. The Junction Creek Campground is a great base camp for those looking to spend a few days in the area. The campground has forty-four sites, outhouses, and picnic facilities. The site is managed by the forest service. The road to the campground does close in the winter, so check its website for that information.

From here, the trail continues on an uphill grade until 2.3 miles into the hike, where the trail then descends to the Junction Creek bridge. Reach the bridge at 2.7 miles. Hikers can cross the bridge and continue as the trail moves into a series of switchbacks. The description for this hike ends at the bridge. Turn around here and return to the trailhead and parking area for a 5.4-mile outing.

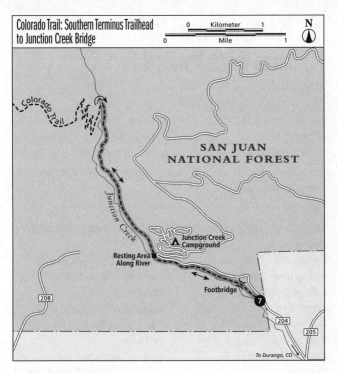

Colorado Trail: Southern Terminus Trailhead to Junction Creek Bridge

Miles and Directions

0.0 From the trailhead, begin hiking northwest on the Colorado Trail.

0.2 Cross a small wooden footbridge.

1.1 Come to a nice rest area on the left (south) side of the trail with great creek access.

1.2 Pass another parking area and trail access point on the right (north).

2.3 After a short ascent, the trail begins descending to the creek.

2.7 Arrive at the Junction Creek bridge. Turn around here to return to the start.

5.4 Arrive back at the parking area and trailhead.

8 Petroglyph Point Trail: Mesa Verde National Park

The Petroglyph Point Trail in Mesa Verde National Park gives hikers a little bit of everything that the park has to offer. Hikers choosing this adventure will see some of the classic cliff dwellings that the park is known for, a beautiful petroglyph panel, and stunning views of the canyons and mesas in the park.

Start: Chapin Mesa Archeological Museum
Distance: 2.9-mile loop
Hiking time: 2 to 3 hours
Difficulty: Moderate due to rugged trail
Trail surface: Packed dirt; rocky
Best season: Spring and fall
Other trail users: None
Canine compatibility: No dogs permitted

Fees and permits: Park entrance fee
Schedule: Open year-round; check website for holiday closures
Maps: USGS Moccasin Mesa CO; trail map available at the visitor center
Trail contact: Mesa Verde National Park, PO Box 8, Mesa Verde, CO 81330; (970) 529-4465; www.nps.gov/meve

Finding the trailhead: From Mancos, Colorado, drive 7.2 miles west on US 160 to the Mesa Verde National Park exit on the right (north). After exiting, turn left (south) onto CO 10, drive 20 miles to the stop sign, and turn right (west) toward the Spruce Tree House Ruins. Continue 0.8 mile to the parking area for the Chapin Mesa Archeological Museum and the Spruce Tree House Ruins. GPS: N37 11.057' / W108 29.306'

The Hike

Mesa Verde National Park is the largest archaeological preserve in the United States. Today the park protects nearly 5,000 known archaeological sites, 600 of which are cliff dwellings. The cliff dwellings of Mesa Verde are some of the most notable and best preserved on the entire North American continent. It is believed that sometime around AD 1200, after living primarily on the mesa top for 600 years, many Ancestral Puebloans began building and living in pueblos beneath the overhanging cliffs and in caves. The structures here range in size from one-room storage units to villages of more than 150 rooms. Cliff Palace, located in the park, is believed to be the largest cliff dwelling ruin in North America. The inhabitants of the dwellings continued to farm the mesa tops as they resided in the alcoves, repairing, remodeling, and constructing new rooms for nearly a century. Researchers say that by the late 1270s, the people in this area began migrating south into present-day New Mexico and Arizona. By 1300 the Ancestral Puebloan occupation of Mesa Verde ended, and all that remains are the ancient ruins.

Some of the most notable and famous ruins within the park include the Balcony House, Cliff Palace, Long House, Mug House, Oak Tree House, Square Tower House, and the ruin visited in this hike: Spruce Tree House. Many of these larger cliff dwellings require a park ranger tour guide for up close views. The Spruce Tree House, however, is open year-round (except for weather, holiday closures, and other administrative closures), and visitors are allowed to hike down to the ruins on their own. A park ranger or two are at the ruins during operating hours to answer questions. The Spruce Tree House is the third largest village in the park and is believed to have been home to around sixty or eighty people. The dwelling has 130 rooms and eight kivas, including a reconstructed kiva that visitors are allowed to climb down into if they so choose.

To begin your hike to the Spruce Tree House and then to Pictograph Point, begin on the paved trail at the southeast corner of the Chapin Mesa Archeological Museum. Just a few feet down the trail you will see your return trail on the left (north). Continue to the right (east) on the paved trail as it begins descending into Spruce Canyon. At 0.2 mile you will reach a trail junction. Stay left (north) to visit the Spruce Tree House Ruins. If the ruins are closed you can turn right (southeast) here onto the Petroglyph Point Trail to bypass the ruins. Heading right (northeast) will skip the ruins and lead to the Petroglyph Point and Spruce Canyon Trails.

The trail to the Spruce Tree House continues north up into the canyon and passes a spring before turning south and arriving at the ruins at 0.3 mile. After your visit to the Spruce Tree House, continue hiking south past the ruins and drop down farther into Spruce Canyon. At 0.4 mile turn left (south) toward the Petroglyph Point and Spruce Canyon Trails. Turn left (east) again at 0.5 mile onto the Petroglyph Point Trail.

Hike up the rock stairs as the Petroglyph Point Trail makes its way to about the midpoint of the canyon wall on the east side of Spruce Canyon. The canyon is littered with Utah juniper, Douglas fir, Gambel oak, and pine. The trail continues to twist and turn along the canyon wall, and even includes a tight squeeze through a couple of boulders and a lot of short ups and downs. Come to a small ruin up in an alcove on the left (east) at 1.2 miles, probably a storage place at one time. Not far beyond, you will arrive at Pictograph

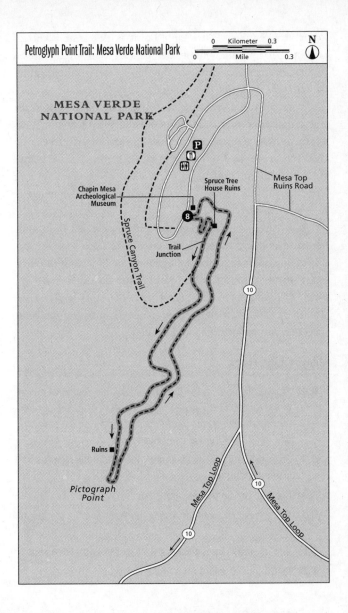

Petroglyph Point Trail: Mesa Verde National Park

MESA VERDE
NATIONAL PARK

Chapin Mesa
Archeological
Museum

Spruce Tree
House Ruins

Mesa Top
Ruins Road

8

Trail
Junction

Spruce Canyon Trail

10

Ruins

Pictograph
Point

Mesa Top Loop

10

10

N

0   Kilometer   0.3

0   Mile   0.3

Point at 1.5 miles. Pictograph Point is the largest known collection of petroglyphs in the park. A trail guide can be purchased at the beginning of the trail or in the visitor center to help you interpret the symbols.

From Pictograph Point the trail continues south for just a short distance as it climbs up the mesa top and turns northeast. Once at the top, follow the trail as it skirts along the canyon rim and offers great views of the canyon below. At 2.3 miles you can get a great view of the canyon as it stretches to the southwest, as well as a view of the museum to the northwest.

At 2.7 miles the trail leaves the pinyon pine and Utah juniper shrubland and turns west to cross over a slickrock section, where you are able to see the Spruce Tree House ruins down below to the southeast. After crossing the slickrock and snapping a few last photos of the ruins, you will return to the paved section of trail. Turn right (west) and return to the trailhead, museum, and parking area at 2.9 miles.

Miles and Directions

0.0 Start hiking east on the paved trail from the southeast corner of the Chapin Mesa Archeological Museum. Pass the dirt-and-rock return trail on the left (north); stay right on the paved trail toward the Spruce Tree House ruins.

0.2 Stay left (north) to visit the ruins; the trail to the right (east) bypasses the ruins.

0.3 Come to the Spruce Tree House ruins. Continue hiking south.

0.4 Turn left (south) onto the Petroglyph Point and Spruce Canyon Trails.

0.5 Turn left (east) up the stairs onto the Petroglyph Point Trail.

1.2 Reach a small set of ruins in the cliff side.

1.5 Arrive at Pictograph Point. The trail climbs to the top of the mesa and turns left (northeast).

2.3 Enjoy nice views of the canyon to the southwest and the museum to the northwest.

2.7 Cross a slickrock area and view the Spruce Tree House ruins down below.

2.9 Turn right (west) back onto the paved trail and arrive back at the trailhead and the Chapin Mesa Archeological Museum.

New Mexico Region

Welcome to the Land of Enchantment! The northwestern New Mexico portion of the Four Corners region is a vast and magnificent area filled with mystery, unusual rock formations, high plains, desert plants, wildlife, and spectacular blue skies. Much of the land is Navajo reservation. The largest city in the Four Corners is in New Mexico: Farmington has a population of nearly 50,000 people and offers the largest variety of shopping in the area. It's a great place to begin your Four Corners adventure. The city itself offers hiking, mountain biking, boating, and fishing right within the city limits. The area has also become an attraction for the film industry, having played host to several full-length films and television episodes.

The highlights of the New Mexico region include mesmerizing rock formations, wind-carved badlands, a dry and arid climate, ancient ruins, and a small collection of natural arches that have been carved out of this rugged and challenging landscape over many, many years. Seven of the trails in this book are found scattered throughout this mysterious area.

In 2013 New Mexico announced more than 1.5 million national park visits, which resulted in more than $81 million in economic benefit for the state from its thirteen National Park Service–managed lands. Only one of those—Chaco

Culture National Historical Park—is included in this guide, but it offers some of the most spectacular ruins in the region. A trip to Chaco Culture National Historical Park will have visitors wondering to themselves, "How did they do that?"

Other trails found in the New Mexico region are located on Bureau of Land Management land and in the city of Farmington. Many of the trails and attractions in the New Mexico region tend to be not well known. Developments like trailhead signs may be few or even nonexistent at some locations. However, if you enjoy having great trails mostly to yourself, the lack of development won't be an issue at all, as you may find yourself the only one on the trail. That being said, use caution in some areas as even the trails may be undeveloped; you will need to have a good sense of direction and to be familiar with using a map and compass. Hiking here has many opportunities, and looks to be getting better!

9 Dancing Horse Trail: Four Corners Monument

It doesn't seem right to not include a hike at the Four Corners Monument in a guide to hiking the Four Corners, so here it is. The 1.5-mile round-trip Dancing Horse Trail offers a short and fairly easy hike in New Mexico and Colorado to a mesa that offers great views of the San Juan River as well as the surrounding area.

Start: Four Corners Monument parking area

Distance: 1.5 miles out and back

Hiking time: 1 to 2 hours

Difficulty: Moderate due to rocky terrain

Trail surface: Dirt trail and rocky path

Best season: Spring and fall

Other trail users: Horseback riders

Canine compatibility: Leashed dogs permitted

Fees and permits: Fee to enter the monument

Schedule: Open year-round

Maps: USGS Teec Nos Pos AZ-CO-NM-UT

Trail contact: Navajo Nation Parks and Recreation, PO Box 2520, Window Rock, AZ 86515; (928) 871-6647; www.navajonation parks.org/htm/fourcorners.htm

Finding the trailhead: From Teec Nos Pos, Arizona, drive north on US 160 for 5.6 miles. Turn left (northwest) onto NM 597/Four Corners Road and drive 0.4 mile to the parking area. GPS: N36 59.935'/W109 2.710'

The Hike

What would a guide to the Four Corners be without a hike at the actual Four Corners Monument? The Four Corners

Monument marks the quadripoint in the southwestern United States—and the only place in the United States where four states meet at such a point—where the states of Arizona, Colorado, New Mexico, and Utah meet. The monument also marks the boundary between two Native American governments, the Navajo Nation reservation and the Ute Mountain Ute Tribe reservation.

The monument is maintained by the Navajo Nation Parks & Recreation department and consists of a large area that has been finished with very nice stonework and then surrounded by a set of vendor stands. During peak tourist season these stands will be filled with local Navajo and Ute artists displaying their art for sale and other vendors selling souvenirs and food. A debate that started many years ago about whether the monument is in the correct location still lingers today. Many people say that the boundary lines are off, and more than likely, with the technology used back in the day to determine these lines, this is probably true. Those that are really nitpicky about the exact point can probably search for and discover the right location, but your photos won't be quite as nice as the ones being taken at the monument.

The monument does require a fee to enter and does have a few amenities. In addition to the vendors, there is a large RV parking and picnic area, as well as a couple of restrooms in the New Mexico quadrant. This is also the location of the Dancing Horse Trailhead. We started the hike for this description from the actual monument, though.

From the Four Corners Monument, begin hiking south and then east through the parking and picnic area. At the eastern end of the picnic area, at 0.2 mile, is a sign for the Dancing Horse Trail. Follow the trail as it turns southeast and heads directly for a mesa that stretches across the New

Mexico and Colorado border. The area looks almost volcanic with all the dark rocks lying around. You'll reach a small saddle at 0.3 mile while still in New Mexico where the trail system offers a few options. Turn right (southwest) to take in the views at the Short Hair and San Juan River overlooks at 0.4 mile before backtracking to the main trail to continue your hike. Turn right (northeast) back onto the main trail and continue hiking gradually uphill along the ridge of the mesa.

Pass the Slowman Point on the left (northwest) at 0.6 mile as the trail gets a bit steeper and the footing becomes a bit more uncertain. As you reach the top of the mesa, you will cross over into Colorado and continue hiking northeast

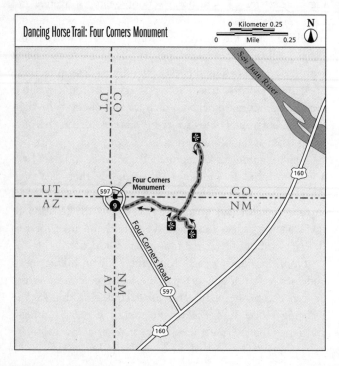

Dancing Horse Trail: Four Corners Monument

until the mesa ends at 0.8 mile. Turn around here and return to the parking area and monument at 1.5 miles.

Miles and Directions

0.0 Start at the Four Corners Monument and begin hiking south and then east through the picnic area.

0.2 At the east end of the picnic area, pick up the trail and continue hiking east.

0.3 Come to a saddle and turn right (south) to visit the Short Hair and San Juan River overlooks.

0.4 Reach the San Juan River overlook.

0.5 Return to the main trail and turn right (northeast).

0.6 Pass the Slowman Point on the left (northwest).

0.8 The trail ends at the end of the mesa. Return to the parking area via the same route.

1.5 Arrive back at the parking area.

10 Anasazi Arch Trail: Bureau of Land Management

New Mexico is not as well known for its arches as nearby Utah. However, arches like Anasazi Arch are nothing to shrug your shoulders at. The very short hike to the arch requires a drive out into the New Mexico oil fields, some rock scrambling, and even a little route finding. What seems like a short and sweet hike requires a little effort that is well worth it. Hikers with an adventurous spirit can explore for hours after locating the arch.

Start: Trailhead parking area
Distance: 0.5 mile out and back
Hiking time: About 1 hour
Difficulty: Moderate due to rock scramble
Trail surface: Dirt and sand
Best season: Year-round
Other trail users: Horseback riders
Canine compatibility: Leashed dogs permitted

Fees and permits: None
Schedule: Open year-round
Maps: USGS Cedar Hill NM
Trail contact: Bureau of Land Management, 6251 College Blvd., Ste. A, Farmington, NM 87402; (505) 564-7600; www.blm.gov/ nm/st/en/fo/Farmington_Field _Office.html

Finding the trailhead: From Aztec, New Mexico, drive north on US 550 for 10.8 miles. Turn left (west) onto CR 2300 and drive 1.3 miles. Stay right at the Y intersection onto CR 2310. Drive 2.8 miles on CR 2310 and turn right onto the unsigned road just past a series of oil and gas facilities. Drive 0.2 mile on the dirt road while keeping to the left (gas and oil installations on the right) to the parking area. GPS: N36 59.764'/W107 54.627'

The Hike

Northwestern New Mexico offers a wealth of natural and cultural history. This remote and rarely visited landscape may not be on the radar of many outdoor enthusiasts, but it should be. Sites like Chaco Culture National Historical Park, Aztec Ruins National Monument, and Salmon Ruins offer glimpses into the lives of the Ancestral Puebloans, the people who called this region home nearly 1,000 years ago. The frigid waters of the San Juan River offer some of the best fly-fishing in the country. The few mountain bike trails, such as the Alien Run Trail, are fun and fast. Hikers willing to explore areas that are off-trail will find a vast array of hiking opportunities.

One sight that you will not want to miss is the Anasazi Arch, also referred to as the Cox Canyon Arch. This natural arch is located north of Aztec, New Mexico, near the Colorado/New Mexico state line. A rough "trail" leads to this beautiful sandstone arch. Visitors should be capable of basic route-finding skills, and be ready and willing to do a little rock scrambling to reach the arch. The arch itself is a lovely and delicate shape, slightly wider than it is tall. Particularly stunning at sunset and sunrise, the nearly 40-foot-tall arch is a worthy destination in and of itself; although most hikers will find it nearly impossible not to explore the trailless landscape that surrounds it.

From the small, unsigned parking area, begin hiking north into the rocky wash. Use a large, prominent rock spire near the trailhead and parking area as a landmark to confirm you are indeed in the right canyon.

Follow the well-worn but unmarked footpath that skirts along the northern edge of this small box canyon. The arch is not visible at the trailhead, but after a very short distance, it will come into view on the northeast horizon. There are three areas that require hand-and-foot-style rock scrambling. While you will not need ropes or specialized climbing equipment, we recommend hiking this trail with a partner, particularly if you have not hiked this area before.

The first small cliff you will encounter is approximately 5 feet tall. Look for good hand- and footholds and, if possible, have your hiking companion spot you. Continue northeast, hiking up-canyon. After a very short distance, you will again need to do some hand-and-foot-style rock scrambling. Less confident climbers will be happy to have a companion to spot their moves in this section. The first section is an easy scramble of about 4 feet onto a small ledge that leads to the top of the cliff. The next scramble is also about 4 feet. This

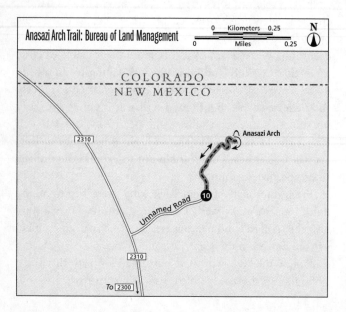

one is more exposed, but has several chiseled hand- and foot-holds to help you along the way. Remember, you will have to climb down this section on your return trip.

Once out of the wash, hike northeast a short distance to the arch. Keen eyes may spot several rock cairns or footprints of previous visitors along the way. Come to the Anasazi Arch at 0.25 mile. Some will find this a perfect destination. Others will be compelled to further explore the large rock shelf where the arch is located before returning to the parking area via the same route. Rumor has it that there is another arch or two on this shelf!

Miles and Directions

0.0 From the parking lot, begin hiking north into the wash to the left of the large rock spire.

0.1 Follow the well-worn footpath up and out of the box canyon into another wash. A bit of rock scrambling is required.

0.2 Hike up and out of the wash to the right (northeast).

0.25 Arrive at Anasazi Arch. Return to the trailhead and parking area via the same route.

0.5 Arrive back at the parking area.

11 Simon Canyon Ruin Trail: Bureau of Land Management

For the best views hike the Simon Canyon Ruin Trail during prime fall foliage season. Don't be fooled, though; this 1.8-mile out-and-back hike offers some great views year-round. Hikers who make their way to the Simon Canyon Ruin will not only get extraordinary views of the canyon and ruin, but they may also catch glimpses of birds of prey that circle the canyon in this area.

Start: Simon Canyon trailhead and parking area
Distance: 1.8 miles out and back
Hiking time: 1 to 2 hours
Difficulty: Easy
Trail surface: Rock and dirt
Best season: Spring and fall
Other trail users: None
Canine compatibility: Leashed dogs permitted

Fees and permits: None
Schedule: Open year-round
Maps: USGS Archuleta NM
Trail contact: Bureau of Land Management, 6251 College Blvd., Ste. A, Farmington, NM 87402; (505) 564-7600; www.blm.gov/nm/st/en/fo/Farmington_Field_Office.html

Finding the trailhead: From Aztec, New Mexico, drive east on NM 173 for 17.3 miles to CR 4280. Turn left (north) onto CR 4280 and drive 3.1 miles to the Simon Canyon parking area and trailhead. GPS: N36 49.403' / W107 39.618'

The Hike

The Simon Canyon Ruin Trail is located in the Simon Canyon Area of Critical Environmental Concern and is near

Navajo Lake State Park. The area is about 3,900 acres in size and allows a few forms of recreation including fishing, hiking, and backpacking. The parking area and trailhead is nicely developed with plenty of parking space, a vault toilet, and a picnic area. There is also access to the San Juan River Trail from this point. The quality waters of the San Juan River, located very nearby, attract fishing enthusiasts from all over the United States. Several full-service guiding companies are located along the river, and in some cases also offer lodging. The river flows right by the mouth of Simon Canyon, where the trailhead is located.

This sandstone canyon has steep to very steep, as well as rough and broken, terrain. The landscape here consists of shrubs; cacti; cottonwood trees found near the water source running through the canyon; pinyon and juniper trees; and even some ponderosa pine up on the higher sections of the canyon rim. The diverse canyon landscape provides habitat for a variety of bird and mammal species as well. Wildlife such as golden eagle, prairie falcon, great horned owl, porcupine, beaver, and deer can all be spotted in or above the canyon.

Because of all that the canyon provides, humans have been able to live in the area as well. Simon Canyon Ruin is a Navajo *pueblito* and sits up high on the eastern side of the canyon overlooking the drainage. The ruin dates back to 1754 and is unique because it sits so far north of the San Juan River, which is considered to be the border between the Navajo and the Ute tribes. The ruin is a one-room structure built on top of a large boulder. The inhabitants notched hand- and footholds high up on the boulder and used a log to reach the holds from the ground. A rope was tied to the log so they could pull the log up when enemies were around.

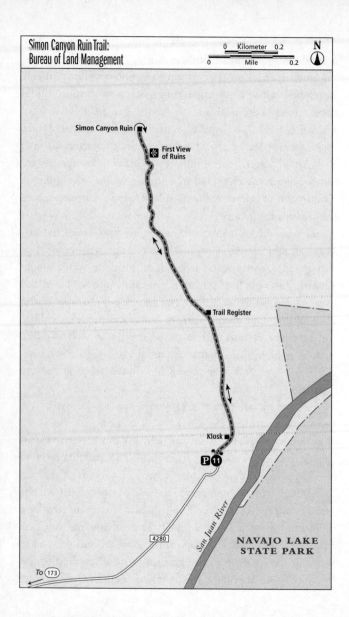

Simon Canyon Ruin Trail:
Bureau of Land Management

0   Kilometer   0.2

0   Mile   0.2

N

Simon Canyon Ruin

First View
of Ruins

Trail Register

Kiosk

P 11

San Juan River

4280

To 173

NAVAJO LAKE
STATE PARK

From the Simon Canyon parking area and trailhead, begin hiking northeast through the gate that keeps vehicles from driving into the wash. Once in the wash at 0.1 mile, you will come to the Navajo Lake State Park and San Juan River Trail sign. Turn left (north) here to begin hiking up the right (east) side of the wash, where the footpath becomes more evident. The trail leaves the wash to the right (east), travels up a two-wheel-drive road, and passes an oil and gas rigging station. Just past the station at 0.3 mile is the trailhead register and a sign that indicates "Foot Trail." From here the trail follows the rim of the canyon on the east side. There are numerous places to walk to the edge of the canyon and look for wildlife or just enjoy the scenery. In the fall the cottonwoods provide a spectacular fall foliage show.

After a short hike you will arrive at the Simon Canyon Ruin at 0.9 mile. A small interpretive sign has been placed near the ruin. Please respect the area and do not attempt to climb the boulder and reach the ruin. Turn around here and return to the trailhead and parking area via the same route.

Miles and Directions

0.0 Begin by hiking northeast through the gate at the north end of the parking area.

0.1 After hiking down into a wash, you will come to a Navajo Lake State Park and San Juan River Trail sign. Turn left (north) to hike up onto the east rim of Simon Canyon.

0.3 Come to a "Foot Trail" sign and trail register.

0.9 Arrive at the Simon Canyon Ruin. Return to the trailhead and parking area via the same route.

1.8 Arrive back at the parking area.

12 Angel Peak Trail: Bureau of Land Management

Discover the mystery of the Angel Peak Scenic Area and the Four Corners' version of the badlands. The beauty of the landscape will amaze hikers visiting this magical area. This 1.6-mile out-and-back hike takes hikers along a narrow ridge and out into badlands for amazing views of Angel Peak. Photographers should consider an evening/sunset hike to capture the perfect picture.

Start: Gate at the northeast corner of the pavilion
Distance: 1.6 miles out and back
Hiking time: 1 to 2 hours
Difficulty: Easy
Trail surface: Dirt path
Best season: Spring and fall
Other trail users: None
Canine compatibility: Leashed dogs permitted

Fees and permits: None
Schedule: Open year-round
Maps: USGS Huerfanito Peak NM
Trail contact: Bureau of Land Management, 6251 College Blvd., Ste. A, Farmington, NM 87402; (505) 564-7600; www.blm.gov/nm/st/en/fo/Farmington_Field _Office.html

Finding the trailhead: From Bloomfield, New Mexico, drive south on US 550 for about 15 miles to CR 7175. Turn left (east) onto CR 7175 and drive 6.2 miles to the pavilion located at the eastern part of the scenic area and campground. GPS: N36 32.919'/W107 51.597'

The Hike

Managed by the Bureau of Land Management, Angel Peak Scenic Area is approximately 10,000 acres of rough and rugged desert landscape ripe for exploration. Hikers and photographers alike will find this little-known area quite exciting. While there are very limited established trails, there are plenty of hiking options along the canyon rim.

Located near Bloomfield, New Mexico, and rising up nearly 7,000 feet, Angel Peak is considered a landmark in the area. The monolith can be seen from quite a distance in any direction. While the peak itself is quite impressive, the surrounding badlands are equally scenic. Bands of yellow, gray, and maroon sandstone, siltstone, and mudstone color the deeply eroded fingers of Kutz Canyon, a sight that is most striking at dusk when the setting sun brings out hues of red, purple, and blue.

The exposed canyon walls reveal a story that is millions of years old. Where there is now only rock and dirt, there were once rushing rivers, grasslands, marshes, lakes, and thick forests. Fossil records indicate that turtles and crocodiles, as well as fish, lizards, and mammals, once thrived here.

As the landscape suggests, Angel Peak and the surrounding area is prone to extreme weather. Snow in the winter, searing heat in the summer, and strong canyon winds in almost any season can be expected here. Steep drop-offs, loose rocks along the rim, and rattlesnakes are other potential hazards. Pay attention to where you step and you'll be fine! Additionally, as on much of New Mexico's public lands, there are several operating pumping jacks and other oil field machinery here. Stay well away from this machinery.

There is a (free) campground here, along with sheltered picnic facilities, grills, and vault toilets. No water is available.

While there are lots of opportunities for off-trail or dispersed hiking here, there are basically two trails. A short nature trail connects two picnic areas. The trail described here is more of a worn path that follows the canyon rim and then traverses an exposed ridge into the canyon. It is scenic and dramatic and well worth the trip to this somewhat remote location.

From the picnic pavilion located at the northeastern part of the scenic area and campground, locate the trail leading northeast toward the rim of the canyon. Almost immediately the trail crosses a cattle guard/gate and follows the rim of the canyon east.

At 0.2 mile the trail leaves the canyon rim and turns to the west to follow a ridgeline partway into the canyon. Come to a very narrow ridge at 0.4 mile and follow the path

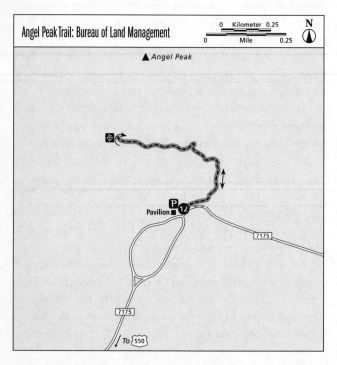

along the ridge between two smaller monoliths. Circumvent the second monolith and continue on to the third monolith at 0.8 mile. From here enjoy the view, and then return to the trailhead and parking area via the same route.

Miles and Directions

0.0   Locate the trail at the northeast corner of the pavilion and hike east through the gate.

0.2   The trail leaves the canyon rim and turns west.

0.4   Reach a very narrow ridge between two of the three rock formations.

0.8   Reach the third peak. Return to the trailhead and parking area via the same route.

1.6   Arrive back at the trailhead.

13 Peñasco Blanco Trail: Chaco Culture National Historical Park

This day hike through the New Mexico desert is a great little getaway. The 7.6-mile out-and-back hike in Chaco Canyon includes petroglyphs, pictographs, Chacoan ruins, and possibly some elk sightings. An early-morning or late-evening hike would be ideal should you choose to hike in the summer months as the midday heat can be intense in the desert canyon.

Start: Pueblo del Arroyo parking area and trailhead
Distance: 7.6 miles out and back
Hiking time: About 5 hours
Difficulty: Moderate due to length and slight elevation gains
Trail surface: Dirt and sand path
Best season: Early spring and late fall for cooler temperatures and wildflowers
Other trail users: Cyclists for the first mile

Canine compatibility: Leashed dogs permitted
Fees and permits: Park entrance fee
Schedule: Open year-round; check website for closures
Maps: USGS Pueblo Bonito NM; trail map available at the visitor center
Trail contact: Chaco Culture National Historical Park, PO Box 220, Nageezi, NM 87037; (505) 786-7014; www.nps.gov/chcu

Finding the trailhead: From Bloomfield, New Mexico, drive 39 miles south on US 550 to CR 7900. Turn right (south) onto CR 7900 and drive 5 miles; then turn right (southwest) onto CR 7950. Drive 16 miles on CR 7950 to the park entrance. From the park entrance continue another 6.7 miles on the one-way loop through the park (NM 57) to the Pueblo del Arroyo parking area and trailhead. GPS: N36 3.752' / W107 57.934'

The Hike

Chaco Culture National Historical Park is home to some of the most exceptional pueblos in the Southwest. The park is located in the Four Corners region in northwest New Mexico in a remote canyon. It contains the most sweeping collection of ancient ruins north of Mexico and preserves one of the United States' most important pre-Columbian cultural and historical areas.

Between 900 and 1150 AD, it is believed that Chaco Canyon was a major center of culture for the Puebloan people. The Chacoans chiseled and shaped sandstone blocks and hauled wood from great distances to build what were at the time the largest buildings in North America. The advanced architectural skills of the people are undeniable, as many of the buildings look to have been aligned to capture the solar and lunar cycles. This type of skill requires years upon years of astronomical observations and centuries of skillfully coordinated construction. Most likely climate change caused the Chacoans to eventually abandon the canyon, beginning with a 50-year drought believed to have occurred in the 1100s.

The Chacoan cultural sites are fragile, and park managers fear that erosion caused by tourists could continue to damage what is left of some of the ruins. Because of this, some sites have been permanently closed, and others may see seasonal closures. The sites are sacred to the Hopi and Pueblo people; therefore, tribal representatives work closely with the National Park Service to share their knowledge and ensure respect for the heritage of the Chacoan culture.

To visit the Peñasco Blanco Ruins, begin hiking northwest from the Pueblo del Arroyo parking area on the Peñasco Blanco Trail. The first section of this trail allows bike riders as

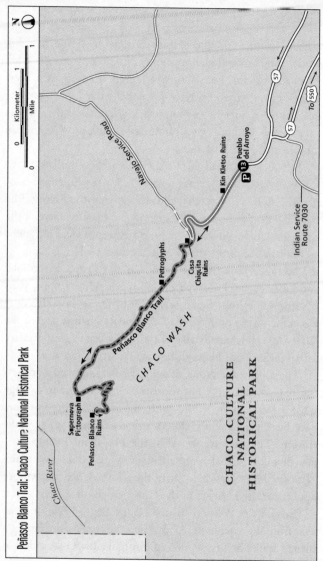

Peñasco Blanco Trail: Chaco Cultura National Historical Park

N

0 1 Kilometer
0 1 Mile

Chaco River

Supernova Pictograph

Peñasco Blanco Ruins

Peñasco Blanco Trail

Navajo Service Road

CHACO WASH

Petroglyphs

Casa Chiquita Ruins

Kin Kletso Ruins

Pueblo del Arroyo

P 13

CHACO CULTURE NATIONAL HISTORICAL PARK

Indian Service Route 7030

To 550

57

57

well, so the dirt and sand trail is wide to accommodate both. At 0.2 mile pass the Kin Kletso Ruins and the right (north) turn to the Pueblo Alto Trail. Continue hiking to the left (northwest) toward the Peñasco Blanco Ruins.

Follow the trail as it travels along the base of the wash wall and comes to the Casa Chiquita Ruins at 1.0 mile. The bike trail ends at this point as well, and the trail narrows to a small footpath. At 1.5 miles you will arrive at a spur trail option. Turn right (north) onto the Petroglyph Trail and follow it as it parallels the main trail and takes you up to the canyon wall for an up close look at some of the petroglyphs in the park. The Petroglyph Trail rejoins the Peñasco Blanco Trail at 1.8 miles. Turn right (northeast) back onto the main trail and continue hiking as the trail crosses the canyon.

After crossing from the right side of the canyon to the left side, you will reach the Chaco Wash. Depending on the season, there may not be much water in the wash. Cross the wash at 2.9 miles, and reach the west side of the canyon wall and the Supernova Pictograph at 3.0 miles. The trail turns south and then switchbacks up the canyon wall before turning north again for the final approach to the ruins. Reach the Peñasco Blanco Ruins at 3.8 miles. The ruins are large and open for people to walk through. Please respect this sacred area and do not harm any of the ruins. Once you are finished exploring, return to the trailhead and parking area via the same route.

Miles and Directions

- **0.0** From the Pueblo del Arroyo parking area and trailhead, begin hiking northwest on the Peñasco Blanco Trail.
- **0.2** Pass the Kin Kletso Ruins on the right (north).

1.0 Reach the Casa Chiquita Ruins on the right (north). The bike trail ends here, and the trail narrows to foot traffic only.

1.5 Turn right (north) onto the Petroglyph Trail to see petroglyphs.

1.8 Turn right (northwest) back onto the Peñasco Blanco Trail.

2.9 Come to and cross the Chaco Wash.

3.0 Pass the Supernova Pictograph on the right (west).

3.8 Arrive at the Peñasco Blanco Ruins. Turn around and return to the trailhead and parking area via the same route.

7.6 Arrive back at the trailhead and parking area.

14 Pueblo Alto Trail: Chaco Culture National Historical Park

This 5.6-mile lollipop hike is a moderate stroll from the Chaco Canyon floor to the canyon rim. The hike along the Pueblo Alto Trail will take hikers to several scenic overlooks of Chaco Canyon as well as views of a unique set of stairs that have been carved into the canyon wall. Be sure to check the park website for closures that may occur during flash flood seasons.

Start: Pueblo del Arroyo parking area and trailhead
Distance: 5.6-mile lollipop
Hiking time: 3 to 4 hours
Difficulty: Moderate due to length
Trail surface: Dirt, sand, and rock
Best season: Early spring and late fall for cooler temperatures
Other trail users: Cyclists for the first mile
Canine compatibility: Leashed dogs permitted

Fees and permits: Park entrance fee
Schedule: Open year-round; check website for closures
Maps: USGS Pueblo Bonito NM; trail map available at the visitor center
Trail contact: Chaco Culture National Historical Park, PO Box 220, Nageezi, NM 87037; (505) 786-7014; www.nps.gov/chcu

Finding the trailhead: From Bloomfield, New Mexico, drive 39 miles south on US 550 to CR 7900. Turn right (south) onto CR 7900 and drive 5 miles; then turn right (southwest) onto CR 7950. Drive 16 miles on CR 7950 to the park entrance. From the park entrance continue another 6.7 miles on the one-way loop through the park (NM 57) to the Pueblo del Arroyo parking area and trailhead. GPS: N36 3.752'/W107 57.934'

The Hike

The Pueblo Alto Trail offers some of the best views of Chaco Canyon. Nearly half of this trail allows hikers an opportunity to walk along the canyon rim. In addition to the canyon views, hikers can see some of the ruins that lie above the canyon. Before this hike, take some time to listen to one of the Park Rangers during an interpretive session and you may hear the unbelievable story of how historians believe all the trees used to build the ruins were delivered to the site. As you hike along the Chacoan Road, the story will seem more and more impossible.

To visit the Pueblo Alto Ruins, begin hiking northwest from the Pueblo del Arroyo parking area on the Peñasco Blanco Trail. The first section of this trail allows bike riders, so the dirt and sand trail is wide to accommodate them.

At 0.2 mile reach the Kin Kletso Ruins and the right (north) turn onto the Pueblo Alto Trail. Begin hiking up a rocky section of trail that looks like it will go right up to the canyon wall and end, but actually passes through a narrow passageway where a large slab of sandstone has broken away from the main wall. After making your way up through the passage, follow the trail as it travels southeast along the rim of Chaco Canyon.

At 1.1 miles you will come to the Pueblo Bonito Overlook and turn left (northeast) onto the Pueblo Alto Trail to begin the loop portion of the hike. The trail continues northeast, higher and higher onto the mesa top, climbing over the sandstone benches. At 1.4 miles reach the Chacoan Steps. Archaeologists uncovered these steps back in the 1970s and came to the conclusion they had been carved out by the Chacoans to make travel back and forth easier.

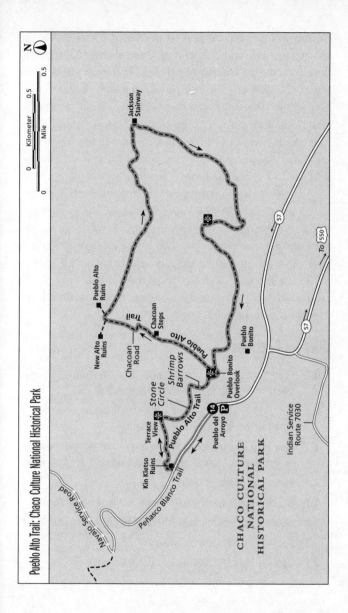

Pueblo Alto Trail: Chaco Culture National Historical Park

N

0   0.5   Kilometer
0   0.5   Mile

Jackson Stairway

Pueblo Alto Ruins

New Alto Ruins

Chacoan Road

Chacoan Steps

Pueblo Alto Trail

Shrimp Barrows

Stone Circle

Terrace View

Pueblo Alto Trail

Kin Kletso Ruins

Peñasco Blanco Trail

Navajo Service Road

Pueblo del Arroyo

Pueblo Bonito

Pueblo Bonito Overlook

14   P

CHACO CULTURE
NATIONAL
HISTORICAL PARK

Indian Service Route 7030

57

57

To 550

You will arrive at the first set of ruins at 1.7 miles. On the left (west) are the New Alto Ruins, and then at 1.8 miles, to the north, are the Pueblo Alto Ruins. From the Pueblo Alto Ruins, the trail turns southeast and begins to make its way back to the Chaco Canyon rim, which you will continue to hike along until you reach the Jackson Stairway at 2.7 miles. The stairway was carved into the canyon wall for access from the canyon floor up to the rim. You probably won't be too interested in trying them out when you see them!

After the Jackson Stairway the trail turns south, and then southwest, to drop onto a lower shelf along the canyon rim before turning northwest and making its way back to the trailhead. On the return you will arrive at a great overlook for Pueblo Bonito on the canyon floor below at 3.7 miles.

Reach the end of the loop portion of the hike at 4.5 miles. Stay left (northwest) to return to the trailhead and parking area at 5.6 miles.

Miles and Directions

0.0 From the Pueblo del Arroyo parking area and trailhead, begin hiking northwest on the Peñasco Blanco Trail.

0.2 Turn right (northeast) at the Kin Kletso Ruins and then stay right (northeast) on the Pueblo Alto Trail.

1.1 Reach the Pueblo Bonito Overlook and turn left (northeast) on the Pueblo Alto Trail to begin the loop portion of the hike.

1.4 Reach the Chacoan Steps.

1.7 Reach a spur trail to the left (west) to the New Alto Ruins.

1.8 Reach a spur trail to the left (north) to the Pueblo Alto Ruins.

2.7 Come to the Jackson Stairway.

3.7 Come to an overlook area for Pueblo Bonito.

4.5 The loop portion of the trail ends. Stay left (northwest) to return to the trailhead and parking area.

5.6 Arrive back at the trailhead and parking area.

15 Bisti/De-Na-Zin Wilderness: Bureau of Land Management

This 4-mile out-and-back hike in the Bisti/De-Na-Zin Wilderness Area will have you wondering, "How did I get here?" The Bisti is full of mystery and wonder, and will keep hikers, adventurers, rock hounds, and history buffs busy for hours and even days. The area is a hidden treasure in northwestern New Mexico that locals have been able to keep to themselves for many years. Be sure to take plenty of water for your trip.

Start: Bisti/De-Na-Zin Wilderness parking area and trailhead
Distance: 4.0 miles out and back
Hiking time: 2 to 3 hours
Difficulty: Easy
Trail surface: Sand and dirt wash
Best season: Spring and fall for cooler temperatures
Other trail users: None
Canine compatibility: Leashed dogs permitted
Fees and permits: None

Schedule: Open year-round
Maps: USGS Alamo Mesa East NM
Trail contact: Bureau of Land Management, Farmington Field Office, 6251 College Blvd., Ste. A, Farmington, NM 87402; (505) 564-7600; www.blm.gov/nm/st/en/prog/blm_special_areas/wilderness_and_wsas/wilderness_areas/bisti.html

Finding the trailhead: From Farmington, New Mexico, drive 43.5 miles south on NM 371 to CR 7500. Turn left (east) and drive 13.5 miles to the Bisti/De-Na-Zin Wilderness Area parking and trailhead on the left (north). GPS: N36 18.738'/W108 0.168'

The Hike

Get ready for an adventure on this hike! The Bisti/De-Na-Zin Wilderness is an otherworldly place located 40 miles south of Farmington. Managed by the Bureau of Land Management, the area consists of 41,170 acres of badlands.

Sandstone, shale, and mudstone, along with coal and silt, make up the majority of the geological features here. The incredible sandstone rock spires, or hoodoos, are the result of weathering and erosion. Rock colors range from maroon to gray to yellow, and turn vivid shades of red, purple, and blue at sunset. In addition to the awe-inspiring geology of the area, there is a rich cultural and paleontological history. Petroglyphs depicting cranes have been found near here, as well as petrified logs and dinosaur fossils. One thing the area does not have is a lot of trails. There are several trailheads, but visitors should be ready to use basic route-finding techniques, along with GPS or map and compass skills.

From the Bisti/De-Na-Zin Wilderness Area parking lot and trailhead, begin hiking north through the sagebrush plain. At 0.2 mile the trail drops down into the wash and enters the badlands. Turn left (southwest) at 0.7 mile and follow the wash. At 1.2 miles turn right (northwest) and follow the trail up and out of the wash. Cross through a smaller wash at 1.4 miles. Come to a pale gray landscape that can only be described as "moonlike" and continue northwest. At 2.0 miles reach a grassland area. This makes a good spot to turn around; return to the trailhead and parking area via the same route.

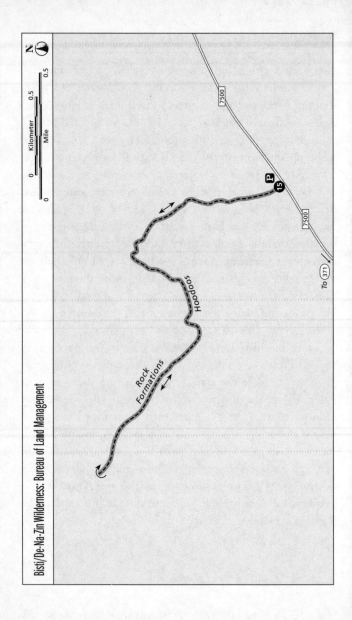

Miles and Directions

0.0 From the Bisti/De-Na-Zin Wilderness Area parking and trail-head, begin hiking north across the sagebrush plain.

0.2 The trail begins dropping down into the wash and badlands.

0.7 Turn left (southwest) and walk in the wash.

1.2 Turn right (northwest) and follow the trail up out of the wash.

1.4 The trail crosses through a smaller wash.

1.8 Cross through an area that is very moonlike.

2.0 Reach a grassy prairie. Turn around here and retrace your steps to the parking area and trailhead.

4.0 Arrive back at the trailhead and parking area.

Utah Region

Welcome to adventure! The southeastern Utah portion of the Four Corners region is filled with large natural bridges and arches, deep and narrow canyons, and towering mountain ranges. Part of the land is Navajo reservation, but a majority of the area is open to public use. Mountain biking, canyoneering, rock climbing, whitewater rafting, kayaking, horseback riding and, of course, hiking are all wonderful recreational opportunities in this region. As in northeastern Arizona, stores and restaurants in the small towns scattered throughout the area can be sparse.

Visitors to the area may find themselves driving and/or hiking in a hot desert environment with little to no water in some places. Be prepared by bringing plenty of water and food into this area if you intend to stay outside and away from the few towns.

The highlights of the Utah region include classic, beautifully colored rock formations, a dry and arid climate, ancient ruins, and fantastic canyons that have been carved out of this rugged and challenging landscape over many years. Five of the trails in this book are found scattered throughout this mountain and canyon area.

When people think of southeastern Utah, Moab is usually a common city mentioned, and for good reason. Moab is a gateway to adventure in Utah, and even though it is pushing the outer limits of the Four Corners region, we had to include hikes around the city in this guide. National parks in the area included in this guide are Arches National Park and Natural Bridges National Monument. Other parks nearby include Capital Reef National Park, Bryce Canyon National Park, Canyonlands National Park, and Grand Staircase–Escalante National Monument. The other trails found in the Utah region are located on Bureau of Land Management land.

Hikers choosing routes from the Utah region of this guide will find themselves exploring canyons and hiking along rivers that offer world-class rafting and kayaking. They will also make their way to classic destinations like Delicate Arch in Arches National Park and to less-known ruins in remote areas. Dust off your hiking shoes, grab your climbing rope and gear, load up your mountain bike, and grab all your map sets, because southeastern Utah can keep adventure seekers busy for a long, long time.

16 House on Fire Ruin Trail: Bureau of Land Management

This pleasant, easy day hike follows the course of upper Mule Canyon, one of the most accessible canyons in the Cedar Mesa region. The 2-mile out-and-back hike travels past great bulging cliffs of Cedar Mesa sandstone that embrace the canyon, which supports an interesting mixture of pinyon-juniper and montane forest environments.

Start: Bridge that crosses Mule Canyon wash
Distance: 2.0 miles out and back
Hiking time: About 2 hours
Difficulty: Easy
Trail surface: Dirt, sand, and rock
Best season: Early spring and late fall
Other trail users: Horseback riders
Canine compatibility: Leashed dogs permitted

Fees and permits: Day-use fee and permit
Schedule: Open year-round
Maps: USGS Hotel Rock UT and South Long Point UT; National Geographic Trails Illustrated #706
Trail contact: Bureau of Land Management, Monticello Field Office, 365 N. Main St., Monticello, UT 84535; (435) 587-1500; www.blm.gov/ut/st/en/prog/more/cultural/archaeology/places_to_visit/mule_canyon.html

Finding the trailhead: From Blanding, Utah, follow US 191 south for 3 miles to the junction of US 191 and UT 95. Turn right (west) onto UT 95 and drive 19.3 miles to the signed turnoff for San Juan CR 263 (Arch Canyon). After turning northeast onto San Juan CR 263, pass a parking area and fee station on the right (south) side of the road. Descend a short but rough and rocky downgrade to the bridge spanning Mule Canyon, 0.3 mile from UT 95. A turnout on the right (south) side of CR 263 has room for two to three cars. GPS: N37 32.245'/W109 43.917'

The Hike

The trail in Mule Canyon is sandy but well worn and easy to follow, with few obstacles, making it passable even to novice hikers. You will see several well-preserved Anasazi ruins should you continue to hike farther into the canyon, most of them grain storage structures. This hike leads directly to some of the ruins that are a very popular site for photography. Please respect these fragile ancient structures.

From the bridge spanning Mule Canyon wash, follow the obvious trail northwest that descends abruptly to the floor of the shallow canyon. The trail quickly leads to the trailhead register and an informational kiosk. Beyond the register the well-defined trail follows the edge of the Mule Canyon arroyo, soon crossing the usually dry wash to the grassy bench on the opposite side. The canyon is quite shallow at this point, flanked by low walls of Cedar Mesa sandstone. Pinyon and juniper trees cover the north-facing slopes to your left. On south-facing slopes the woodland is open and sparse.

After about 0.5 mile, where the wash begins a northwest trend, the canyon grows increasingly confined by bulging walls that rise 150 feet to the rims above. Soon, with slick-rock underfoot, you begin to follow the floor of the wash. Multiple trails appear frequently in this part of the canyon, but the way is straightforward—you simply follow the wash. The woodland vegetation in the sheltered confines of the canyon is rich and well developed, more typical of a higher and wetter environment. The northwest trend of the canyon allows considerable shade to be cast by the canyon walls, reducing heat, sunlight, and evaporation.

At 1.0 mile you will reach the House on Fire Ruin on the right (north). The ruins are small and sit midway up the canyon wall. House on Fire Ruin earned its name because when photographed at the right time of the day, the canyon wall above the ruins looks like flames shooting out of the top of the ruins. During most of the year, if you plan your hike to arrive at the ruins around 10 a.m. and get the right camera setting and camera angle, you can capture the perfect photo.

Return to the parking area and trailhead via the same route.

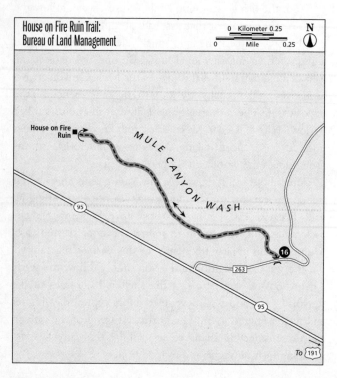

Miles and Directions

0.0 From the bridge crossing the Mule Canyon wash, begin hiking northwest along the trail.

0.5 The canyon becomes more confined.

1.0 Arrive at House on Fire Ruin. Return to the trailhead and parking area via the same route.

2.0 Arrive back at the parking area and trailhead.

17 Sipapu and Kachina Bridges Loop Trail: Natural Bridges National Monument

This memorable 5.8-mile half-day loop hike surveys the two largest of the natural bridges in the monument, separated by the dramatic bulging Cedar Mesa sandstone cliffs of White Canyon. The trail passes Horse Collar Ruins, an example of an unusual style of Anasazi architecture, and loops back to the Sipapu Bridge trailhead via the mesa top, giving hikers the entire spectrum of the monument's landscape.

Start: Sipapu Bridge parking area and trailhead

Distance: 5.8-mile loop

Hiking time: 4 to 5 hours

Difficulty: Moderate due to elevation gain and terrain

Trail surface: Rock, sand, slickrock, and dirt

Best season: Spring and fall

Other trail users: None

Canine compatibility: No dogs permitted

Fees and permits: Park entrance fee

Schedule: Open year-round; check website for closure dates

Maps: USGS Moss Back Butte UT; trail map available at the visitor center

Trail contact: Natural Bridges National Monument, HC-60 Box 1, Lake Powell, UT 84533; (435) 692-1234; www.nps.gov/nabr

Finding the trailhead: From Blanding, Utah, drive 3.9 miles south on US 191 and turn right (west) onto UT 95. Drive west on UT 95 for 30.2 miles to UT 275, signed for "Natural Bridges National Monument." Turn right (north) onto UT 275 and drive 7.2 miles to the Sipapu Bridge parking area and trailhead. GPS: N37 36.799'/W110 0.554'

The Hike

A visit to Natural Bridges National Monument is a must for anyone traveling on UT 95 across Cedar Mesa. Located near the head of White Canyon, the bridges in the monument are among the largest in the world.

From the Sipapu Bridge trailhead, the trail begins as a slickrock route, descending over the White Canyon rim. The way quickly evolves into a constructed trail, carved into the slickrock, with steps in places that afford better footing. Once below the rim, the trail traverses beneath an overhang to the top of a steel stairway at 0.1 mile that allows passage over an otherwise impassable cliff band. Soon you reach a second stairway that offers an exciting passage over a 20-foot cliff. Just below the stairway, descend a tall, sturdy wooden ladder at 0.2 mile, and then follow the trail as it curves out to a fine viewpoint on a sandstone ledge at 6,000 feet, overlooking Sipapu Bridge. The trail then descends steadily.

Descend two short but steep slickrock friction pitches, with the aid of handrails and two short ladders, at 0.6 mile, and then reach level ground beneath the bridge in the White Canyon wash about 0.7 mile from the trailhead. This bridge, the largest in the monument, is no longer being enlarged by stream erosion, since its abutments now rest high above the wash. In its dimensions Sipapu is second only to Rainbow Bridge in Arizona's Glen Canyon National Recreation Area, and thus bears the distinction of being the second longest natural bridge in the world.

To continue, cross the seasonal stream beneath the towering span of Sipapu and follow the well-worn trail southwest, crossing the wash three more times en route to Deer Canyon. The trail is a delightful walk through spectacular

White Canyon. Deer Canyon opens up on the right (north) 1.3 miles from the trailhead. Don't miss the short side trip to Horse Collar Ruins at 1.5 miles, just below the mouth of Deer Canyon. A steep, slick rock scramble is necessary to reach the deep alcove that houses an unusual collection of small Anasazi dwellings and granaries.

Resuming your trek down-canyon on the well-defined trail, you will cross the wash five more times en route to Kachina Bridge. Hike under Kachina Bridge at 3.1 miles. The trail continues southbound, now ascending the White Canyon tributary of Armstrong Canyon.

At 3.3 miles and just beyond Kachina Bridge, reach the trail to the canyon rim and the Kachina Bridge parking area. Turn left (east) to begin hiking up the east side of the canyon wall. After a brief slickrock ascent ends, traverse a short distance to a signed junction at 3.4 miles. The trail to the right (south) continues ascending Armstrong Canyon, eventually leading to Owachomo Bridge. Bear left (southeast) toward the Kachina Bridge parking area.

The trail ascends, steeply at times, via rock steps and a series of short, tight switchbacks. Reach the parking area and road at 3.9 miles. The trail resumes on the opposite (east) side of the road, winding over the mesa top on a gradual uphill. At 4.8 miles turn left (north) at the signed junction, heading toward the Sipapu Bridge trailhead. Turning right (south) will take you to the Owachomo Bridge parking area and trailhead. The trail descends 120 feet into a prominent draw carved into the mesa, and then steadily ascends the cairned route across the slickrock. Once to the top of the climb, it is just a short distance to the Sipapu Bridge trailhead at 5.8 miles.

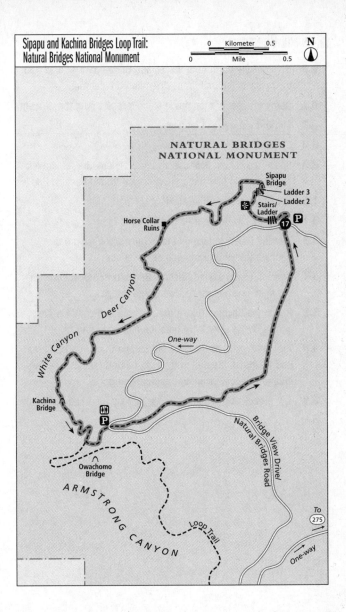

Sipapu and Kachina Bridges Loop Trail:
Natural Bridges National Monument

0 Kilometer 0.5

0 Mile 0.5

N

NATURAL BRIDGES
NATIONAL MONUMENT

Sipapu
Bridge

Ladder 3

Ladder 2

Stairs/
Ladder

17 P

Horse Collar
Ruins

Deer Canyon

White Canyon

One-way

Kachina
Bridge

P

Owachomo
Bridge

ARMSTRONG CANYON

Loop Trail

Bridge View Drive/
Natural Bridges Road

To
275

One-way

Miles and Directions

0.0 Begin hiking north from the Sipapu Bridge parking area and trailhead as the trail drops down into the canyon.

0.1 Come to a set of man-made stairs to assist with the descent.

0.2 Climb down a set of ladders.

0.6 Climb down a set of ladders.

0.7 Reach the canyon floor directly under Sipapu Bridge. Turn left (southwest) to hike through the canyon toward Kachina Bridge.

1.5 Reach the Horse Collar Ruins.

3.1 Continue hiking under Kachina Bridge.

3.3 Turn left (east) to hike up out of the canyon toward the Kachina Bridge parking area and overlook.

3.4 Stay left (east) toward Kachina Bridge overlook. The trail to the right (west) leads to Owachomo Bridge.

3.9 Reach the Kachina Bridge parking area and continue east across Bridge View Drive onto the mesa-top trail.

4.8 Turn left (north) to return to the Sipapu Bridge parking area and trailhead. The trail to the right (south) leads to the Owachomo Bridge parking area and trailhead.

5.8 Arrive back at the Sipapu Bridge parking area and trailhead.

18 Negro Bill Canyon Trail: Bureau of Land Management

The 4.6-mile round-trip Negro Bill Canyon Trail is a gem located very close to downtown Moab. As if the drive to the trail along the Colorado River wasn't enough, the trail takes hikers to the 243-foot-long Morning Glory Natural Bridge. The bridge is the sixth longest in the United States. During early spring hikers might consider bringing a pair of sandals or water shoes as the trail crosses the year-round stream numerous times along the hike.

Start: Negro Bill Canyon parking area and trailhead

Distance: 4.6 miles out and back

Hiking time: 3 to 4 hours

Difficulty: Easy

Trail surface: Rock, sand, and dirt

Best season: Spring and fall

Other trail users: None

Canine compatibility: Leashed dogs permitted

Fees and permits: None

Schedule: Open year-round

Maps: USGS Moab UT; National Geographic Trails Illustrated #501

Trail contact: Bureau of Land Management Moab Field Office, 82 E. Dogwood, Moab, UT 84532; (435) 259-2100; www .blm.gov/ut/st/en/fo/moab/ recreation/hiking_trails/negro _bill_canyon.html

Finding the trailhead: From Moab, Utah, drive 3.1 miles east on UT 128 to the parking area and trailhead on the right (south). GPS: N38 36.586' / W109 32.014'

The Hike

This 4.6-mile round-trip hike starts just above the banks of the Colorado River east of Moab and travels up scenic

Negro Bill Canyon. The hike ends at a stunning 243-foot-long natural bridge, the sixth largest natural rock span in North America. Remember, the bridge is located in the second side canyon on the right, not in Negro Bill Canyon.

One of the best things about this hike is that the fairly level trail to Morning Glory Bridge ascends just over 200 feet along the way. The singletrack trail begins to the left of a year-round stream that produces plentiful plant life in Negro Bill Canyon, and the steep walls of the canyon provide plenty of shade in the early morning and late afternoon. There is a pit toilet and plenty of parking at the well-maintained parking area.

Begin hiking southeast on the trail through the thick plant life along the creek, and reach the trail register at 0.4 mile. In case you are wondering about all this greenery in the canyon—yes, there is poison ivy.

Continue along the east bank of the shallow creek. At 1.1 miles you'll come to the first of many creek crossings. Not to worry: Unless you're hiking during or right after a lot of rain, the creek crossings are pretty tame. Most of the crossings have well-placed rocks for hopping, and many hikers will be able to jump over several of the crossings.

After you cross the creek for the fifth time, follow the trail as it turns east at 1.3 miles to stay in Negro Bill Canyon. The canyon to the right (south) is Abyss Canyon. Proceed east in the main canyon as the trail climbs uphill for just a short stretch and then drops back down to the creek to cross a few more times.

At 1.9 miles cross the creek for the ninth time, and follow the trail southeast as it leaves Negro Bill Canyon and enters a side canyon. The trail climbs up to a shelf on the left (north) side of the canyon and will continue along this

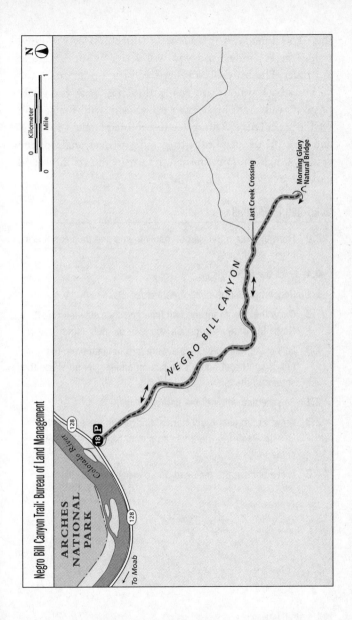

shelf. You'll get your first views of Morning Glory Natural Bridge at 2.1 miles, and you will arrive at the bridge at 2.3 miles. The canyon ends here, and the bridge spans the canyon's back wall. If you weren't looking for it, you could possibly walk right by because it blends in with the canyon wall so well. This is a fun place to explore, so take your time and take plenty of photos to get the perfect angle of the bridge. Once you are finished, return to the trailhead and parking area via the same route.

Miles and Directions

0.0 From the Negro Bill Canyon parking area and trailhead, begin hiking southeast.

0.4 Pass the trail register.

1.1 Reach the first of many stream crossings.

1.3 Cross the stream for the fifth time and then stay left (east) in Negro Bill Canyon. Abyss Canyon is to the right (south).

1.9 Follow the trail across the stream for the ninth time. The trail heads southeast into a side canyon and climbs up above the stream to the left.

2.1 See the first views of the natural bridge.

2.3 Arrive at Morning Glory Natural Bridge and the end of the canyon. Return to the trailhead and parking area via the same route.

4.6 Arrive back at the trailhead and parking area.

19 Corona Arch Trail: Bureau of Land Management

This spectacular hike is a 2.2-mile out-and-back route that leads to a very recognizable and well-known arch in the Moab area. The hike requires some rock scrambling in a couple of areas, but is still an ideal hike for families. Hikers will also get to see a second arch, Pinto Arch (Bow Tie Arch), which tends to be overshadowed by the size and beauty of Corona Arch (known by some as Rainbow Arch).

Start: Corona Arch parking area and trailhead
Distance: 2.2 miles out and back
Hiking time: 1 to 2 hours
Difficulty: Moderate due to a rock-scrambling section
Trail surface: Rock, sand, slick-rock, and dirt
Best season: Spring and fall
Other trail users: None
Canine compatibility: Leashed dogs permitted

Fees and permits: None
Schedule: Open year-round
Maps: USGS Moab UT; National Geographic Trails Illustrated #500
Trail contact: Bureau of Land Management Moab Field Office, 82 E. Dogwood, Moab, UT 84532; (435) 259-2100; www .blm.gov/ut/st/en/fo/moab/ recreation/hiking_trails/corona _arch_trail.html

Finding the trailhead: From Moab, Utah, turn (south) onto UT 279 and drive 10 miles to the parking area and trailhead on the right (east). GPS: N38 34.466'/W109 37.940'

The Hike

So many hikes in the Moab area culminate with a big "wow," and the Corona Arch Trail will not let you down if you're expecting that "wow" factor at the end. However, because of its proximity to Arches National Park, Corona Arch tends to be a little less known. This 2.2-mile trail travels over a slickrock landscape that has been well marked with cairns, making it easy to follow. From the trailhead the trail gains over 400 feet in elevation.

Begin hiking southwest on the Corona Arch Trail from the parking area and trailhead. The trail quickly scrambles up the canyon wall and arrives at the trail register and some train tracks at 0.1 mile. After crossing the railroad tracks continue north, follow an old eroded roadbed through a gap in the slickrock bench above.

Once you reach the top of the canyon wall, follow the trail northeast toward the base of a large sandstone wall. After you reach the wall and follow the base, you'll come to a safety cable at 0.7 mile that protects this slightly exposed section of trail. From this point on, Corona Arch is visible. Follow the rock cairns across the slickrock after the first safety cable until you reach another safety cable, and then a ladder, at 0.8 mile. This cable and ladder will probably be a little tougher to navigate than the first cable.

From the top of the steps that have been carved along the second cable to help hikers, climb the short ladder up over a ledge and follow the cairns up to the top of a large bench. From this point on, the hike is pretty straightforward, with Corona Arch looming in front of you. Before you rush over to Corona Arch, don't forget to stop and check out Bow Tie Arch at 1.0 mile on the left (north).

Arrive at Corona Arch at 1.1 miles. Once you are finished enjoying the views, return to the trailhead and parking area via the same route.

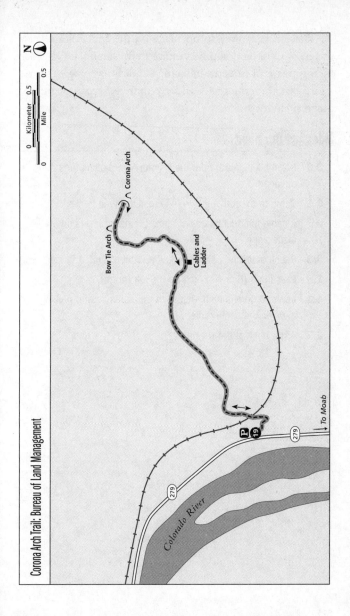

Corona Arch Trail: Bureau of Land Management

Bow Tie Arch

Corona Arch

Cables and Ladder

P
19

To Moab

279

279

Colorado River

N

Kilometer 0.5

Mile 0.5

There is very little to no shade on this hike. Please keep this in mind should you be visiting in the summer. Consider hiking this trail in early morning or early evening. Also, be aware that the cables and ladder require a certain degree of physical ability.

Miles and Directions

0.0 Begin hiking north from the Corona Arch parking area and trailhead.

0.1 Come to the trail register and cross the train tracks.

0.7 A cable handrail has been placed to assist hikers on the rocky slope.

0.8 Reach a second cable handrail and then climb a ladder.

1.0 Pass Pinto (Bow Tie) Arch on the left (north).

1.1 Arrive at Corona Arch. Return to the trailhead and parking area via the same route.

2.2 Arrive back at the trailhead.

20 Delicate Arch Trail: Arches National Park

This 3.4-mile out-and-back hike in Arches National Park is considered a classic and is probably the most popular hike in the park. Delicate Arch sits 1.7 miles from the trailhead and attracts numerous park-goers because of its sheer beauty and uniqueness. The hike includes a long section of slickrock hiking in the middle and at the end, which makes for a fun hike.

Start: Wolfe Ranch parking area and Delicate Arch trailhead

Distance: 3.4 miles out and back

Hiking time: 2 to 3 hours

Difficulty: Moderate due to terrain and modest elevation gain

Trail surface: Sand, dirt, slickrock, and rock

Best season: Spring and fall

Other trail users: None

Canine compatibility: No dogs permitted

Fees and permits: Park entrance fee

Schedule: Open year-round; check website for closure dates

Maps: USGS The Windows Section UT; National Geographic Trails Illustrated #211; trail map available at the visitor center

Trail contact: Arches National Park, PO Box 907, Moab, UT 84532; (435) 719-2299; www.nps.gov/arch

Finding the trailhead: From Moab, Utah, drive north on US 191 for 4.6 miles to the park entrance/Arches Scenic Drive. Turn right (north) into the park and drive 12.3 miles to Delicate Arch Road. Turn right (east) onto Delicate Arch Road and continue 1.3 miles to the Wolfe Ranch parking area and Delicate Arch trailhead on the left (north). GPS: N38 44.138'/W109 31.241'

The Hike

It may not be the largest, widest, or most remote arch in Utah, but Delicate Arch is arguably one of the most beloved and unforgettable arches in the region. Its shape graces the state's license plate, and thousands of people of all ages and nationalities make the 3.4-mile round-trip trek to see this remarkable feature each year. If you're seeking a bit of desert solitude, you might still find it at Delicate Arch—very early in the morning, on a weekday, in the off-season. Otherwise, be prepared to share the trail.

From the Delicate Arch trailhead, begin hiking east toward Wolfe Ranch. Wolfe Ranch is the former homestead of John Wesley Wolfe and his family, who settled in the area in the late 1800s to raise cattle. There is an interpretive trail guide for the 0.25 mile Wolfe Ranch Trail available at the trailhead and visitor center that details life for the Wolfe family as well as the trials of living in the desert.

Cross a footbridge over Salt Wash at 0.1 mile and turn left (north) to visit a small cluster of petroglyphs at 0.2 mile. After viewing these interesting petroglyphs—noticing that the art portrays figures on horseback, which gives clues as to when this rock art may have been created—continue southeast to rejoin the trail to Delicate Arch.

The trail gradually begins to climb, coming to a large slickrock slab at 0.9 mile. "Slickrock" is a term that refers to the "petrified" sand dunes that are so common in the Four Corners region. The trail follows a cairn-lined slickrock path to a somewhat narrow ledge. Follow the ledge a short distance before reaching Delicate Arch at 1.7 miles. Take in all the scenic beauty of this special area—where else can you enjoy a 50-foot red sandstone arch and a view of the

Delicate Arch Trail: Arches National Park

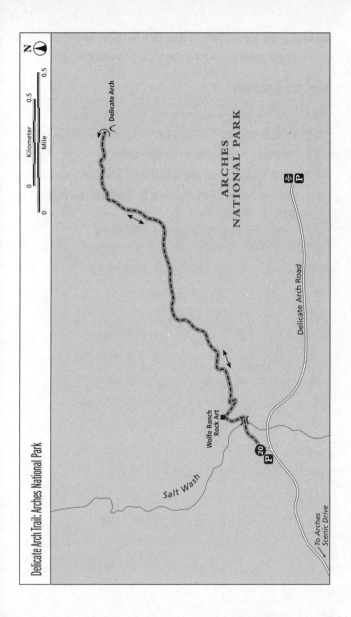

snow-capped La Sal Mountains at the same time? Return to the trailhead and parking area via the same route.

Miles and Directions

0.0 From the Delicate Arch trailhead, begin hiking east.

0.1 Cross a footbridge and turn left (north) to view petroglyphs.

0.2 Reach the petroglyphs on the left (north).

0.9 The trail approaches and then crosses a large slickrock slab.

1.7 Arrive at Delicate Arch. Return to the trailhead and parking area via the same route.

3.4 Arrive back at the trailhead and parking area.

Dehydration

Have you ever hiked in hot weather and had a roaring headache and felt fatigued after only a few miles? More than likely you were dehydrated.

Symptoms of dehydration include fatigue, headache, and decreased coordination and judgment.

When you are hiking, your body's rate of fluid loss depends on the outside temperature, humidity, altitude, and your activity level. On average, a hiker walking in warm weather will lose four liters of fluid a day. That fluid loss is easily replaced by normal consumption of liquids and food.

However, if a hiker is walking briskly in hot, dry weather and hauling a heavy pack, he or she can lose one to three liters of water *an hour*. It's important to always carry plenty of water and to stop often and drink fluids regularly, even if you aren't thirsty.

About the Authors

JD Tanner grew up playing and exploring in the hills of southern Illinois. He has earned a degree in outdoor recreation from Southeast Missouri State University and an advanced degree in outdoor recreation from Southern Illinois University in Carbondale. He has traveled extensively throughout the United States and is the director at Touch of Nature Environmental Center.

Emily Ressler-Tanner grew up splitting time between southeastern Missouri and southeastern Idaho. She spent her early years fishing, hiking, and camping with her family. In college she enjoyed trying out many new outdoor activities and eventually graduated from Southern Illinois University in Carbondale with an advanced degree in recreation resource administration.

Together they have climbed, hiked, paddled, and camped all over the United States. They co-instructed college-level, outdoor recreation courses for several years before joining the staff at the Leave No Trace Center for Outdoor Ethics as Traveling Trainers. Former residents of Farmington, New Mexico, JD and Emily now reside in southern Illinois.

FalconGuides they have written or revised include:

Best Easy Day Hikes Grand Staircase-Escalante (revised)
Best Easy Day Hikes Missouri Ozarks
Best Easy Day Hikes Springfield, Missouri
Best Easy Day Hikes St. Louis
Best Hikes Near St. Louis